WITHDRAWN
NDSU

# FOUR
# FINNS
✡ ✡ ✡ ✡

J. K. Paasikivi

# FOUR FINNS

✡ ✡ ✡ ✡

**Political Profiles by
MARVIN RINTALA**

UNIVERSITY OF CALIFORNIA PRESS
BERKELEY AND LOS ANGELES, 1969

DK
461
m32
R5
1969

University of California Press
Berkeley and Los Angeles, California
Cambridge University Press
London, England
Copyright © 1969 by
The Regents of the University of California
Library of Congress Catalog Card Number: 69-12461
Designed by Steve Reoutt
Printed in the United States of America

To my parents,
and four other Finns—
my grandparents
✶✶✶✶

# Acknowledgments
✪ ✪ ✪ ✪

Like every author, I am indebted to a large number of persons, ranging from librarians to typists. Many friends and critics in Finland and the United States have, I trust, enriched my knowledge of Finnish politics. All these persons, willingly or not, are contributors to the pages that follow. For the inscribed photograph of K. J. Ståhlberg, I am indebted to Kustannusosakeyhtiö Tammi and, especially, Mrs. Linda Tanner; for all the other photographs, I am grateful to the Finnish Foreign Ministry, from whose archives they come.

Most of all, however, I should like to record my debt to the late Sigmund Neumann, who, years ago, introduced me to the study of leadership. He was an incomparable master and friend, and he will undoubtedly forgive any of my arguments which lack his imprimatur. As Zarathustra spoke, one repays a teacher badly if one always remains nothing but a pupil. One also repays a teacher badly, nevertheless, if one forgets that in the beginning was the pupil.

# Contents
✪ ✪ ✪ ✪

|     |                                                      |     |
| --- | ---------------------------------------------------- | --- |
| I   | Four Men Among Many                                  | 1   |
| II  | The Aristocrat in Politics: Gustaf Mannerheim        | 13  |
| III | The Bureaucrat in Politics: Väinö Tanner             | 47  |
| IV  | The Scholar in Politics: K. J. Ståhlberg             | 71  |
| V   | The Politician in Politics: J. K. Paasikivi          | 93  |
| VI  | Finnish Politics as a Vocation                       | 113 |

# I
✧✧✧✧
## Four Men Among Many

It could be argued that thought, action, and organization are the three basic aspects of politics. All men think something about politics, if only to conclude that they should reject it completely. They make some kind of comparative evaluation of existing and ideal political systems. This evaluation in turn motivates political action. Those who decide, as do conservatives, that the existing political system is either completely or virtually ideal act, either peacefully or violently, to defend the existing system. Those who decide, as do progressives, that some other political system would be better than the existing system act, either peacefully or violently, to change the existing system. Those who decide that all political systems are equally worthwhile decide, in effect, that there is no reason to change the existing system. Those who decide that all political systems are equally undesirable may be active or passive in their anarchism, but even their passivity may have profound political consequences.

When men act in politics, they relate themselves to other men who are also acting, or who have already acted, or who may act in the future, in politics. The most important aspect of these human relationships—and therefore of political organization—is that some men lead and other men follow in politics, as in all other areas of human life. Government by the multitude is a contradiction in terms.[1] It may even be

[1] William Bennett Munro, *Personality in Politics: Reformers, Bosses, and Leaders: What They Do and How They Do It* (New York, 1924), p. 83; Nils Andrén, *Modern Swedish Government* (Stockholm: Almqvist & Wik-

possible to equate politics with leadership, or influencing of leadership, of a state.[2] The necessity of leadership does not mean that only a select few are born leaders, and that the rest belong to the great unwashed.[3] It does not even mean that the same men are always leaders and other men always followers.[4] It does mean that in political systems including millions of persons some men must function as leaders and

sell, 1961), p. 207; Maurice Duverger, *Political Parties: Their Organization and Activity in the Modern State* (translated by Barbara and Robert North, New York, 1963), p. 424. Even an unlikely observer agreed that "It is against the natural order that the greater number should govern, and the smaller number be governed." Jean Jacques Rousseau, *The Social Contract* (edited by Charles Frankel, New York, 1951), p. 59.

[2] Max Weber, "Politics as a Vocation," in H. H. Gerth and C. Wright Mills (editors), *From Max Weber: Essays in Sociology* (New York, 1958), p. 77.

[3] Such arguments have not been confined to Continental Europe. "Leadership, then, in the true sense of the term can only come about by substituting something for the law of natural selection. Great men can only be begotten by great men. Leaders in any sphere of life are not produced by environment, although it may furnish the opportunity. If we permit the racial stock to be impoverished, then we lessen the chance of, or forbid the birth of leaders." William D. Tait, "Psychology, Leadership, and Democracy," *The Journal of Abnormal and Social Psychology*, XXII (April–June, 1927), 30. "The section of any community that produces leaders or genius of any sort is only a minute percentage. . . . This something which we call 'genius' is not a matter of family, but of stock or strain, and is inherited in precisely the same manner as are the purely physical characters. . . . it is race, always race, that produces genius." Madison Grant, *The Passing of the Great Race, or The Racial Basis of European History* (New York, 1924), p. 98. These views do not appear particularly shocking when it is remembered that Sigmund Freud wrote to Albert Einstein: "That men are divided into leaders and the led is but another manifestation of their inborn and irremediable inequality. The second class constitutes the vast majority; they need a high command to make decisions for them, to which decisions they usually bow without demur [sic]. In this context we would point out that men should be at greater pains than heretofore to form a superior class of independent thinkers, unamenable to intimidation and fervent in the quest for truth, whose function it would be to guide the masses dependent on their lead." Robert A. Goldwin, Ralph Lerner, and Gerald Stourzh (editors), *Readings in World Politics* (New York, 1959), pp. 29–30.

[4] Alvin W. Gouldner (editor), *Studies in Leadership: Leadership and Democratic Action* (New York, 1950), p. 20; Winston S. Churchill, *My Early Life: A Roving Commission* (New York, 1958), p. 47.

other men as followers. The attractiveness of the leader and the attraction of the follower are, nevertheless, the same phenomenon, viewed from different perspectives.[5] This phenomenon obviously involves a special relationship between leaders and followers as the essence of leadership.[6]

Machiavelli observed in the *Discourses* that a multitude without a chief is useless. This is true of both democratic and totalitarian political systems. Almost everyone outside the Soviet Union acknowledges that some men there are indeed more equal than others. It is not always remembered, however, that leadership is inevitably present in democratic political systems as well. There has never been a democracy destitute of leaders. Rather than an absence of leaders, democracies may be characterized by multiplicity of leaders, and by the refusal of followers to give to any one leader a continuous enough allegiance.[7] Even in the smallest direct democracies, where the need for representation does not arise, there is leadership.[8] There are always those (leaders) who exercise power over followers, and those others (fol-

[5] Charles Edward Merriam, *Four American Party Leaders* (New York, 1926), p. x. It seems a sign of conceptual confusion to argue that leaders and followers have the same characteristics, as do Ray C. Hackman and Rexford G. Moon, Jr., "Are Leaders and Followers Identified by Similar Criteria?" *The American Psychologist*, 5 (July, 1950), 312; E. P. Hollander and Wilse B. Webb, "Leadership, Followership, and Friendship: An Analysis of Peer Nominations," *The Journal of Abnormal and Social Psychology*, 50 (March, 1955), 163–167.

[6] One writer sadly relates that "a very able political scientist writing of leadership" discusses "why men obey or do not obey, why they tend to lead or follow, as if leading or following were the essence of leadership." Mary Parker Follett, "Some Discrepancies in Leadership Theory and Practice," in Henry C. Metcalf and L. Urwick (editors), *Dynamic Administration: The Collected Papers of Mary Parker Follett* (New York, 1942), p. 289; see also p. 291.

[7] Ernest Barker, *Reflections on Government* (New York, 1958), p. 140; Woodrow Wilson, *Congressional Government: A Study in American Politics* (New York, 1958), pp. 58–59.

[8] Herbert J. Spiro, *Government by Constitution: The Political Systems of Democracy* (New York, 1959), p. 302; Irving Knickerbocker, "Leadership: A Conception and Some Implications," *The Journal of Social Issues*, IV (Summer, 1948), 29.

lowers) over whom power is exercised by leaders.⁹ This fact was perceived by Emerson:

> Mankind have, in all ages, attached themselves to a few persons, who, either by the quality of that idea they embodied, or by the largeness of their reception, were entitled to the position of leaders and lawgivers.¹⁰

The study of comparative politics is today in need of a clearer understanding of the meaning of leadership in different political systems. There is widespread agreement that leadership is an important aspect of politics, and therefore of the study of politics. What political leadership actually involves, however, is not so clear.¹¹ One important reason for this uncertainty is that relatively little is known about indi-

---

⁹ Elementary as this definition of leadership may seem, a careful student, after surveying the literature of psychology and social psychology, concludes: ". . . in the main, those who write on leadership do not write on power and *vice versa*. . . . we have two separate, practically selfcontained bodies of literature—one on leadership, the other on power." Kenneth F. Janda, "Towards the Explication of the Concept of Leadership in Terms of the Concept of Power," *Human Relations*, XIII (November, 1960), 354. It has even been argued that leadership and power are not related. Robert Bierstedt, "The Problem of Authority," in Morroe Berger, Theodore Abel, and Charles H. Page (editors), *Freedom and Control in Modern Society* (New York, 1954), pp. 70–72. Far superior in its level of understanding is the observation of an unsuccessful novelist that leadership involves power over the thought and action of followers. Benjamin Disraeli, *Coningsby or, the New Generation* (New York, 1961), pp. 135–136. Disraeli's point was made, perhaps less persuasively, by Abraham Myerson, "The Qualities of the Leader and the Follower," in his *The Foundations of Personality* (Boston, 1923), p. 275.

¹⁰ Ralph Waldo Emerson, *Representative Men: Seven Lectures* (Boston, 1876), p. 21. It is difficult to grasp the meaning of the statement that "Politics by leadership is one of the distinguishing features of the twentieth century." Lester G. Seligman, "The Study of Political Leadership," *The American Political Science Review*, XLIV (December, 1950), 904. Equally confusing is the mystical statement: "Personalities always matter in politics, and never have they counted for more than in our century, which has, at one and the same time, tended to collectivize the individual and to individualize collective power." Bertrand de Jouvenel, "Political Science and Prevision," *The American Political Science Review*, LIX (March, 1965), 35.

¹¹ The study of leadership is undoubtedly in somewhat better condition presently, nevertheless, than in 1930, when a profoundly pessimistic conclu-

vidual leaders in many of the smaller political systems. Most students of comparative politics are reasonably familiar with, say, Heinrich Brüning and Léon Blum, but not with Hjalmar Branting [12] and Sir Robert Borden. The latter may be quite as important as the former for purposes of comparative analysis, even though their world-historical significance may have been less. Generalizations about leadership, as well as about other aspects of politics, are thus frequently based upon inadequate data.

It is the purpose of the present study to help fill this gap by comparison of four major leaders of the Finnish political system: Gustaf Mannerheim, Väinö Tanner, K. J. Ståhlberg, and J. K. Paasikivi. The choice of these particular Finnish leaders rather than some others is, of course, a matter of judgment. There are other Finns, such as Kyösti Kallio, P. E. Svinhufvud, and Risto Ryti, who deserve detailed study, but whom the present author finds less interesting both as political leaders and as human beings.[13] Consideration of these latter leaders would introduce men very different from the four Finns discussed in the present study. Kallio, for instance, was an important center party leader who shared most of Ståhlberg's goals, without sharing the latter's intelli-

sion was reached by Harold D. Lasswell, *Psychopathology and Politics* (New York, 1960), p. 2.

[12] Branting has been accurately described as "one of the most successful politicians of modern times in any democratic country, contributing perhaps more than anyone else to the transformation of Sweden in not much more than half a century from a backward and largely agricultural society to one of the most advanced countries in the world." Michael Futrell, *Northern Underground: Episodes of Russian Revolutionary Transport and Communications through Scandinavia and Finland 1863–1917* (London, 1963), p. 35.

[13] Even this list omits the name of Otto Kuusinen, the *alpha* and *omega* of Finnish Communism, who was probably the most powerful Finn who ever lived. Since most of Kuusinen's political career was spent in the Soviet Union, there is some doubt that he was a leader of the Finnish political system *per se*. Furthermore, little is known in detail about his more than four decades in the Soviet Union. Finally, what is known about Kuusinen is well-treated by John H. Hodgson, *Communism in Finland: A History and Interpretation* (Princeton, 1967).

gence and decisiveness. Svinhufvud, vigorous but ignorant, exercised a far different kind of leadership within the National Coalition Party than did Paasikivi.[14] Ryti was a strong-willed liberal who climaxed his political career with a comradeship-in-arms with Adolf Hitler. The picture that this study presents is therefore perhaps more flattering to the Finnish political system than it might have been.

These four Finns were significant, however, as indicated by the offices they held. Three of them—Mannerheim, Ståhlberg, and Paasikivi—served as President of the Republic.[15] Two—Tanner and Paasikivi—were Prime Minister. All except Mannerheim held other influential Cabinet posts. Mannerheim was Commander-in-Chief during three wars. Tanner led the largest Finnish party for almost three decades. Ståhlberg was the chief author of the Finnish Constitution. Paasikivi decided Finnish foreign policy from 1944 to 1956. In a very real sense, the story of these men is the story of Finnish politics in the twentieth century.[16] The strengths and weaknesses of these four Finns were writ large in the lives of four million other Finns, if not in the lives of the rest of the human race.

One crucial problem of democratic political systems is to find followers who can wisely accept or reject the potential

[14] Svinhufvud is one of the major characters in my study, *Three Generations: The Extreme Right Wing in Finnish Politics* (Bloomington, 1962). It is misleading to characterize Svinhufvud as a member of the intelligentsia, as does Leonard Bushkoff, "Revolution and Nationalism: Two Studies on the History of Communism in Eastern Europe," *World Politics*, XV (April, 1963), 498. An early biography by one of Svinhufvud's lieutenants is Erkki Räikkönen, *Svinhufvud: The Builder of Finland* (London, 1938). The first scholarly study is Einar W. Juva, *P. E. Svinhufvud I:1861–1917* (Porvoo: Werner Söderström Osakeyhtiö, 1957); Juva, *P. E. Svinhufvud II:1917–1944* (Porvoo: Werner Söderström Osakeyhtiö, 1961).

[15] Even a highly unsympathetic observer concluded that Tanner's career would have entitled him to be President. Matti Kurjensaari, *Jäähyväiset 50-luvulle* (Helsinki: Kustannusosakeyhtiö Tammi, 1960), p. 102.

[16] *Pääministeri J. W. Rangellin puhe Suomen Marsalkka C. G. Mannerheimin 75-vuotispäivänä* (Helsinki: Kauppalehti Oy:n Kirjapaino, 1942), p. 1.

leaders who came forward.[17] It may well be that a democratic political system is to be judged by its leaders.[18] If so, the case of Finland does not support the assumption of Adolf Hitler that through democracy inferior persons must, almost as a law, become leaders.[19] The optimistic assumptions which the Finnish Constitution makes about holders of institutional office [20] have largely been fulfilled. It is a common expectation among Finns that the right man will be in the right place at the right time.[21] This expectation has not been entirely unjustified, judging from the political careers of these four Finns. It is, no doubt, true that he is great who never reminds us of others,[22] but the great man is at the same time genuinely representative of the deeper needs and tendencies of human nature, so that in following him men truly express themselves.[23] By this standard the four Finns under consideration merit the scholar's respect and attention.

That the large majority of Finns chose to follow men like Mannerheim, Tanner, Ståhlberg, and Paasikivi, rather than, for example, Otto Kuusinen suggests that optimism concerning the future of the Finnish political system is not entirely unjustified. It is misleading to argue that the Finns have

[17] Eric Bentley, *A Century of Hero-Worship: A study of the idea of heroism in Carlyle and Nietzsche, with notes on Wagner, Spengler, Stefan George, and D. H. Lawrence* (second ed., Boston, 1957), p. 263.
[18] Munro, *Personality in Politics*, pp. 93, 114.
[19] *Hitler's Secret Book* (translated by Salvator Attanasio, New York, 1961), p. 30.
[20] Pauli Burman and Matti Nieminen, *Osakeyhtiö Isänmaa* (Jyväskylä: K. J. Gummerus Osakeyhtiö, 1959), p. 151.
[21] *Paasikiven linja II:Juho Paasikiven puheita ja esitelmiä vuosilta 1923–1942* (Porvoo: Werner Soderström Osakeyhtiö, 1956), p. 264; L. A. Puntila, "Svinhufvudin elämäntyön kuvaus valmis," *Historiallinen Aikakauskirja*, 1962 (Number 2), p. 147; "Mitä tähdet lupaavat Suomelle v. 1962," *Helsingin Sanomat*, December 31, 1961; Esteri Paalanen, *Uskon ja teon ihmisiä —Pienoiselämäkertoja koulunuorisoa varten* (Helsinki: Kustannusosakeyhtiö Otava, 1956), p. 42.
[22] Emerson, *Representative Men*, p. 11.
[23] Charles Horton Cooley, *Human Nature and the Social Order* (revised ed., New York, 1922), p. 353.

never had much political instinct, since they have looked to brave or astute leaders to defend them in their unfortunate geographical position.[24] If they indeed followed such leaders, it can hardly be said that they lack political instinct. That, given its undeniably scarce political resources—especially in international politics—the Finnish political system, alone among those created in Europe after the First World War, is still both independent and democratic is due at least partially to the excellence of political leadership in that system. The present study is in large part a success story in the face of enormous odds.

A success story, however, need not run indefinitely. Most students of Finnish politics would probably agree that there are today very few, if any, Finnish political leaders who approach the stature of men as diverse as Mannerheim, Tanner, Ståhlberg, and Paasikivi. As the following pages reveal, none of the latter were averse to exercising power. All four, nevertheless, considered the personal possession of political power less important than the use to which this power was put. All, with the possible exception of Tanner after 1939, were able to take political power or leave it, as evidenced by their voluntary withdrawal from political leadership when the preconditions for their policies seemed nonexistent. It is difficult to imagine any contemporary Finnish political leader yielding power unless absolutely necessary. Furthermore, these four leaders had personal standards of moral integrity which they refused to sacrifice for partisan advantage. If contemporary leaders have such standards, they have kept them well hidden. If Finnish politics is indeed characterized by a paucity of statesmen, as has been claimed by a Communist literary figure,[25] this paucity has become more noticeable with the passage of time.

[24] Eric Dancy, "Finland Takes Stock," *Foreign Affairs*, 24 (April, 1946), 513.
[25] Raoul Palmgren, "Kansan ja herrojen presidentit, vahvat ja heikot presidentit," *Tilanne*, December, 1961, p. 60.

Since each of the four Finns under consideration was a unique individual, a separate chapter is devoted to each. It is not the intention of the present study, however, to provide a comprehensive biography—however brief—of each. Treatment of each is analytical rather than chronological. Furthermore, this analysis is political, not psychoanalytical. These men were not sick, and no useful purpose would be served by trying to prove that they were. These chapters are not life histories in a broader sense, for only a limited range of the experiences of these men—that which is explicitly political—is treated in detail. The student of politics is properly concerned with the human being as politician, not with the politician as human being. The latter subject can safely be left to the journalists—Freudian and otherwise. More significant an omission than childhood fantasies is the omission of any attempt to picture the nonpolitical professional careers of these men. Mannerheim as a military strategist, Tanner as a cooperative manager, Ståhlberg as a scholar, Paasikivi as a banker—all these are interesting stories but essentially extraneous to the task at hand. That each of these men had a particular "private" career substantially influenced, of course, his political thought and action, as well as his chances for political leadership. Whether Mannerheim, for example, understood the "proper" role of tanks in modern warfare is, nevertheless, of secondary importance in understanding his political career.[26]

[26] A Finnish literary figure has argued that Mannerheim had an impact upon the fate of Finland solely as a soldier. Jussi Talvi, *Elän Venäjän varjossa—Kertomus olemassaolontaistelusta* (Helsinki: Kustannusosakeyhtiö Otava, 1959), p. 316. If Mannerheim was indeed not a significant figure in Finnish politics, his inclusion in the present study would be unjustified. Talvi's argument, however strained, is at least intelligible, since Mannerheim clearly did not get so many followers in Finnish politics as he sought. Another argument—that Mannerheim was free of the will to power—advanced by one of the followers whom Mannerheim *did* obtain approaches the incredible. This claim was made by Lauri Aho, "Ylipäällikkövaltiomies," in V. A. M. Karikoski, H. Kekoni, and A. E. Martola (editors), *C. G. Mannerheim-Suomen marsalkka* (Helsinki: Kustannusosakeyhtiö Kivi, 1951), p. 270. Aho neglects to explain how a man becomes Commander-in-Chief of

The present study, in short, attempts merely to provide profiles of the political careers of these four Finns. A profile is not a well-rounded portrait. Its dimensions are always limited, and its creator may be a caricaturist at heart. Even the caricaturist, however, only exaggerates those features that are already present. Furthermore, a profile, unlike a full-length portrait, seldom reveals feet of clay. There may, indeed, be room even for profiles because scholarly analysis of leadership in the Finnish political system, even by Finnish scholars, is almost totally lacking. The standard introduction to that system, for instance, devotes only one brief paragraph to leadership.[27] Finnish scholars, like so many others, have forgotten that politics is made not only by social forces working through institutions, but by individual human beings as well. The strengths and weaknesses of human

an army and President of a republic while lacking any will to power. The testimony of those who knew Mannerheim best reveals that in him the will to power was unusually strong and well-developed. Paul Rodzianko, *Mannerheim: An Intimate Portrait of a Great Soldier and Statesman* (London, 1940), p. 66; Lauri Malmberg, quoted in Kaarlo Hildén, Ragnar Numelin, and Birger Fagerström (editors), *Sotamarsalkka Mannerheim 75 vuotta kesäkuun 4 päivänä 1942—juhlajulkaisu* (Helsinki: Oy Suomen Kirja, 1942), p. 42; Erik Heinrichs, *Mannerheim Suomen kohtaloissa I:Valkoinen kenraali 1918–1919* (Helsinki: Kustannusosakeyhtiö Otava, 1957), pp. 219–221; Heinrichs, "Mannerheim. Muutamia mietteitä Marsalkan muiston aatepiiristä," in *Peruskalliomme maanpuolustus* (Helsinki: Suomen Reserviupseeriliitto, 1951), pp. 13, 15; Heinrichs, "Kolmen sodan ylipäällikkö," *Uusi Suomi*, January 28, 1951; Stig Jägerskiöld, *Nuori Mannerheim* (translated by Sirkka Rapola, Helsinki: Kustannusosakeyhtiö Otava, 1964), pp. 182, 243; Stig Jägerskiöld, *Gustaf Mannerheim 1906–1917* (translated by Sirkka Rapola, Helsinki: Kustannusosakeyhtiö Otava, 1965), pp. 246, 305. At least early in his presidential term, while his health was still tolerable for an old man, Mannerheim was clearly a "strong" President. Paavo Kastari, *Tasavallan presidentin asema* (Porvoo: Werner Söderström Osakeyhtiö, 1961), pp. 26, 71–72; G. A. Gripenberg, *Lontoo—Vatikaani—Tukholma: Suomalaisen diplomaatin muistelmia* (translated by Lauri Karén, Porvoo: Werner Söderström Osakeyhtiö, 1960), pp. 352–354. A profoundly unfair evaluation of Mannerheim's presidency is given by a Finnish nationalist historian in L. A. Puntila, *Suomen poliittinen historia 1809–1955* (Helsinki: Kustannusosakeyhtiö Otava, 1964), pp. 188–189.

[27] Jaakko Nousiainen, *Suomen poliittinen järjestelmä* (third ed., Porvoo: Werner Söderström Osakeyhtiö, 1967), pp. 97–98.

nature are omnipresent if not omnipotent in politics. That is why political science without biography is a form of taxidermy.[28] If this book brings its subjects back to life, even for a brief moment, it will have served its purpose. The power of scholarly resurrection carries with it considerable responsibility,[29] and it is to be hoped that these profiles are drawn by a hand at least as tolerant of human frailty as it is zealous for truth.

[28] Lasswell, *Psychopathology and Politics*, p. 1.
[29] John A. Garraty, *The Nature of Biography* (New York, 1957), p. 28.

## II
✪✪✪✪
# The Aristocrat In Politics: Gustaf Mannerheim

Gustaf Mannerheim was probably the most famous and the least known modern Finnish political figure.* For three decades he was a leading member of the older generation of conservatives. Twice, during critical postwar periods (1918–1919 and 1944–1946), he served as head of state, first as Regent and then as President. A myth of international proportions grew around his name. Since the Winter War his military genius has been widely recognized. Mannerheim is one of two Finns (the other being Jean Sibelius) of whom most educated Westerners have heard. On his seventy-fifth birthday, in June, 1942, he became the first and undoubtedly last Marshal of Finland; among those visiting Mannerheim's military headquarters that day to offer congratulations was (to use the visitor's own phrase) an unknown soldier from the First World War, Adolf Hitler. Mannerheim, who had been a general in the Great War, was one of the few human beings before whom Hitler showed any signs of humility after 1933. Unlike some other marshals, Mannerheim did not grovel before the former corporal. As they met, Mannerheim stood stiffly as ever while Hitler bowed before him. During the luncheon in the Marshal's honor Hitler's table talk was confined to gracious statements about his host.[1] Hitler was

* An earlier version of this chapter appeared in the *Journal of Central European Affairs*. Permission to draw upon that article is gratefully acknowledged.
[1] Erik Heinrichs, *Mannerheim Suomen kohtaloissa II:Suomen marsalkka* (Helsinki: Kustannusosakeyhtiö Otava, 1959), pp. 317–318; Taru Stenvall,

not the first German ruler to honor Mannerheim. In 1918 Mannerheim had been awarded the Iron Cross; according to the statement of Emperor William II, he was the first foreign military officer who had fought against Germany to receive such recognition.[2]

In the land of his birth Mannerheim was loved and hated intensely. Those whom he led to victory in the Finnish Civil War of 1918 saw him as the chief figure in the attainment of Finnish independence; those whom he defeated in 1918 saw him as the devil incarnate. His supporters considered Mannerheim the greatest Finn of his time,[3] the greatest Finnish soldier,[4] the greatest Finnish leader,[5] or simply the greatest of all Finns.[6] After his death, the League of Finnish Nobles

---

Marski ja hänen "Hovinsa" (Porvoo: Werner Söderström Osakeyhtiö, 1956), pp. 158–159, 164.

[2] Erik Heinrichs, Mannerheim Suomen kohtaloissa I:Valkoinen kenraali 1918–1919 (Helsinki: Kustannusosakeyhtiö Otava, 1957), p. 224n. Well before 1918 William II and Mannerheim had met. Stig Jägerskiöld, Nuori Mannerheim (translated by Sirkka Rapola, Helsinki: Kustannusosakeyhtiö Otava, 1964), pp. 201–202.

[3] Anni Voipio, Suomen Marsalkka—elämäkerta (Porvoo: Werner Söderström Osakeyhtiö, 1953), pp. 8, 378, 405, 424; Heinrichs, Mannerheim, II, 446. At the unveiling of a statue of Mannerheim in 1960, President Urho Kekkonen apparently joined in this evaluation. Helsingin Sanomat, June 5, 1960.

[4] Voipio, Suomen Marsalkka, pp. 12, 319, 387, 405; Heinrichs, Mannerheim, II, 295; H. Holma, "Sotamarsalkka Mannerheim ja diplomatia," in Kaarlo Hildén, Ragnar Numelin, and Birger Fagerström (editors), Sotamarsalkka Mannerheim 75 vuotta kesäkuun 4 päivänä 1942—juhlajulkaisu (Helsinki: Oy Suomen Kirja [1942]), p. 78; Yrjö Blomstedt, "C. G. E. Mannerheim—marsalkka-presidentti," in Matti Kuusi (editor), Suomen tasavallan presidentit (Porvoo: Werner Söderström Osakeyhtiö, 1960), p. 155; W. E. Tuompo and others (editors), Kesäkuun neljäs päivä 1942— Suomen Marsalkan, vapaaherra C. G. Mannerheimin 75-vuotispäivän juhlallisuudet (Helsinki: Kustannusosakeyhtiö Otava, 1942), pp. 6, 18, 127.

[5] Heinrichs, Mannerheim, II, 220; W. E. Tuompo, "Sotilas ja sota päällikkö," in V. A. M. Karikoski, H. Kekoni, and A. E. Martola (editors), C. G. Mannerheim—Suomen marsalkka (Helsinki: Kustannusosakeyhtiö Kivi, 1951), p. 119.

[6] Voipio, Suomen Marsalkka, pp. 12, 309; Tancred Borenius, Field-Marshal Mannerheim (London, 1940), pp. 247, 278; Gustaf Ehrnrooth, "Carl Gustaf Emil Mannerheim-Muistopuhe," in Suomen Aatelisliitto, Suomen Marsalkka Vapaaherra Gustaf Mannerheim. Sotilas—Valtiomies-

proclaimed that Mannerheim was the pride and glory of the Finnish nobility.[7] A Finnish newspaper reported that on the first anniversary of the beginning of the Civil War "Finland's uncrowned king" was followed around the city of Vaasa by throngs of worshipful subjects.[8] Justification for these unqualified endorsements was seen in the fact that Mannerheim was the savior of Finland in three wars: 1918, 1939–1940, and 1941–1944.[9] It seemed that he had been chosen

*Ihminen* (Helsinki: Kustannusosakeyhtiö Otava, 1953), p. 32; Olof Lindeman, "Muistelmia Marsalkan viimeisiltä vuosilta," in *ibid.*, pp. 144, 155; Kai Donner, *Sotamarsalkka vapaaherra Mannerheim* (Porvoo: Werner Söderström Osakeyhtiö, 1937), p. 263; Karikoski, Kekoni, and Martola (editors), *C. G. Mannerheim*, p. 14.

[7] Ehrnrooth, "Carl Gustaf Emil Mannerheim," pp. 9, 24. In view of the fact that this nobility has been dying out since Finland became a republic in 1917 or 1919 (the date depends upon one's preferences in constitutional law), this judgment, at least, is likely to remain unchallenged.

[8] Heinrichs, *Mannerheim*, I, 314–315. An impressionable foreign observer wrote of the Finns at Mannerheim's bier: ". . . they waited their turn to pass by the mortal remains of the valiant spirit who was in a very special sense their uncrowned king." Hudson Strode, *Finland Forever* (new ed., New York, 1952), p. 462.

[9] Borenius, *Field-Marshal Mannerheim*, pp. 170–171, 174, 245; Heinrichs, *Mannerheim*, II, 10; Voipio, *Suomen Marsalkka*, pp. 192, 195–196; Hugo Backmansson, "Hajanaisia muistelmia," in Suomen Aatelisliitto, *Suomen Marsalkka*, p. 86; Wolf. H. Halsti, *Suomen puolustaminen—Suomen puolustuskysymyksen ja puolustus-mahdollisuuksien pääpiirteet. Mitä jokaisen kansalaisen tulisi tietää näistä asioista* (Helsinki: Kustannusosakeyhtiö Otava, 1939), p. 154; W. E. Tuompo and others, *C. G. E. Mannerheim—sotilas, valtiomies, tiedemies, lasten ystävä—lausuntoja Suomen Yleisradiossa 4 VI. 1942* (n. p.: Oy Suomen Yleisradio A.B., n. d.); Urho Toivola (editor), *Introduction to Finland 1960* (Porvoo: Werner Söderström Osakeyhtiö, 1960), p. 100. This was true outside of Finland as well. For instance, Mannerheim was described during the crucial Russo-Finnish negotiations of 1939 as "the one man who won freedom for Finland" in 1918. "The Liberator of Finland Mobilizes Against Russia," *Life*, 7 (October 23, 1939), 22. A few months later, the British public was told that "because of him, Gustaf Mannerheim, Finland was free" in 1918. Paul Rodzianko, *Mannerheim: An Intimate Picture of a Great Soldier and Statesman* (London, 1940), p. 144. In 1960 the United States Government issued two postage stamps bearing Mannerheim's portrait, with the caption "Liberator of Finland." No portrait, however, could match the following silhouette: "What need is there to give him titles or dignities? His name by itself shines like a light in the northern firmament, and flashes as a sword to confound his enemies. For he it is who has made Finland into a nation and given her a future." John Pollock, "Sil-

by God to save his nation; it seemed that divine intervention led the wandering Finn back to his homeland in December, 1917, after three brilliant decades in the Imperial Army of the Russian Emperor.[10] There is no evidence that Mannerheim considered himself the agent of God, but he did state privately that Fate had made him the embodiment of what the Finnish nation needed in 1918–1919.[11]

Not all Finns saw Mannerheim in a favorable light, especially during the interwar decades. For those defeated in the Civil War he remained "the butcher of Finland's workers and farmers."[12] Critics of his large policy of Finnish intervention in the Russian Civil War referred to Mannerheim as Finland's chief warmonger.[13] He was attacked as responsible for Finland's involvement in the Second World War,[14] and venom-

---

houettes in Finland: (I) The Head of the State," *The New Europe,* XI (June 5, 1919), 177. A lady journalist, obviously impressed by "the best-looking man in Europe," announced: "Indeed there is no more splendid figure in world history today, and no greater soldier." Rosita Forbes, *These Men I Knew* (New York, 1940), pp. 273, 276.

[10] Borenius, *Field-Marshal Mannerheim,* p. 115; Voipio, *Suomen Marsalkka,* p. 396; Herman Gummerus, *Sotamarsalkka Mannerheim* (Helsinki: Kustannusosakeyhtiö Otava, 1937), p. vi; Rudolf Walden, in Hildén, Numelin, and Fagerström (editors), *Sotamarsalkka,* p. 17; Blomstedt, "C. G. E. Mannerheim," p. 146. The German Minister to Finland during the Second World War was less charitable in describing Mannerheim's return: "But when Bolshevism came to power in Russia, Mannerheim remembered that he had been born in Finland and returned to Finland." Wipert v. Blücher, *Suomen kohtalonaikoja—Muistelmia vuosilta 1935–44* (translated by Lauri Hirvensalo, Porvoo: Werner Söderström Osakeyhtiö, 1950), p. 239. An equally uncharitable comment was made by Marja Niiniluoto, "Mannerheim: hahmo ja sen tulkinnat," *Helsingin Sanomat,* June 4, 1967.

[11] Carl Enckell, "Muutama muistelma yhteistyöstäni Gustaf Mannerheimin kanssa," in Suomen Aatelisliitto, *Suomen Marsalkka,* p. 42; Carl Enckell, *Poliittiset Muistelmani,* II (translated by Heikki Impola, Porvoo: Werner Söderström Osakeyhtiö, 1956), pp. 336, 346.

[12] O. Vilmi, *Fasimi Suomessa—Sen syyt ja tarkoitus* (Leningrad: Valtion kustannusliike kirja, 1931), p. 51; see also Kyllikki Kallas, *Kolmastoista luku —romaani* (Helsinki: Kustannusosakeyhtiö Tammi, 1961), p. 153.

[13] O. H. Puro in Parliament, *Valtiopäivät 1919, Pöytäkirjat,* II, 1357.

[14] A. Äikiä, *Tulikantele-Runoja* (Petrozavodsk: Karjalais-Suomalaisen SNT:n valtion kustannusliike, 1947), p. 91; Heinrichs, *Mannerheim,* II,

ously satirical cartoons depicted his checkered career.[15] Indicative of the mistrust in which his name was held among those defeated in 1918 was the budget request of the Social Democratic Cabinet in 1927: additional government support for General Mannerheim's Child Welfare League would be dependent upon a change in the name of that organization.[16] The Social Democratic Party had vigorously opposed election of Mannerheim to the presidency in 1919 because of his role in the Civil War. It was therefore ironic when, at Mannerheim's state funeral in 1951, the Social Democratic Speaker of Parliament, Karl-August Fagerholm, stated that only the deceased could have led Finland out of war in 1944 without an internal struggle.[17] This was not merely funeral oratory—in 1944 Fagerholm had privately predicted that the election of Mannerheim to the presidency would prove "a blessing to the Fatherland." [18]

Today, largely because of his role in the Second World War, Gustaf Mannerheim has many more admirers in Finland than he had in the interwar decades. In many important respects he is a symbol of the *Volksgemeinschaft* which the Finnish nation experienced during the Winter War. His grave is a national shrine, and yet the substance of his politics remains, as before, shrouded in mystery. If this is true in Mannerheim's homeland, it is doubly so outside of Finland. Mannerheim's politics appear to have confounded most foreign observers. He has been labeled an Anglophile,[19] a

397–398; "Soujeluskuntalainen v:lta 1917," *Suomen marsalkka Mannerheim* (Helsinki: Oy Kirja Präntti Ab, 1960), p. 6.

[15] A. Halonen (editor), *Suomen Luokkasota—Historiaa ja Muistelmia* (Superior, Wisconsin: Amerikan Suom. Sos. Kustannusliikkeiden Liitto, 1928), p. 80.

[16] Heinrichs, *Mannerheim*, I, 389.

[17] Voipio, *Suomen Marsalkka*, p. 401; Heinrichs, *Mannerheim*, II, 460–461. This was also Paasikivi's public evaluation as Mannerheim retired from the presidency in 1946. *Paasikiven linja I—Juho Kusti Paasikiven puheita vuosilta 1944–1956* (Porvoo: Werner Söderström Osakeyhtiö, 1956), p. 69.

[18] Heinrichs, *Mannerheim*, II, 396.

[19] Strode, *Finland Forever*, pp. 193, 440, 462.

Francophile,[20] a Russophobe,[21] a Germanophile,[22] and even a pro-Nazi.[23] His surname has been frequently and mistakenly assumed to be "von Mannerheim," not only by nonscholars,[24] but by authors of scholarly monographs [25] and even in dictionaries.[26]

[20] Borenius, *Field-Marshal Mannerheim*, p. 90; Georg Brandes, "Scandinavian Sympathies and Destinies," *Foreign Affairs*, I (June 15, 1923), 31.

[21] Walter Duranty, *USSR: The Story of Soviet Russia* (Philadelphia, 1944), p. 251. In describing the beginning of the Russo-Finnish War of 1941–1944, an American scholar stated: "In Finland, bloody Baron Mannerheim, put in power by German arms in 1918, launched his war of revenge against Russia." Frederick L. Schuman, *Design for Power: The Struggle for the World* (New York, 1942), p. 131. In fact, German arms put P. E. Svinhufvud, not Mannerheim, into power in 1918; it was only the defeat of the Central Powers which made possible Mannerheim's election to the regency in December, 1918. It should further be apparent that Mannerheim had no reason to seek revenge against Russia, which had been very good to him for three decades.

[22] Frederick L. Schuman, *Night over Europe: The Diplomacy of Nemesis 1939–1940* (New York, 1941), p. 399; Gregory Meiksins, *The Baltic Riddle: Finland, Estonia, Latvia, Lithuania—Key-points of European Peace* (New York, 1943), pp. 144–145, 156; Sydney Finkelstein, *Composer and Nation: The Folk Heritage of Music* (New York, 1960), p. 227. During the Winter War a Finnish-born British scholar stated heatedly but correctly that to label Mannerheim pro-German was "utterly baseless, indeed grotesque." Borenius, *Field-Marshal Mannerheim*, p. 137. As an officer in the Russian Imperial Army Mannerheim had shared the conventional anti-German sentiments of his fellow officers. Jägerskiöld, *Nuori Mannerheim*, p. 180; Stig Jägerskiöld, *Gustaf Mannerheim 1906–1917* (translated by Sirkka Rapola, Helsinki: Kustannusosakeyhtiö Otava, 1965), pp. 199, 201, 214–215, 229, 263, 322–323.

[23] Frederick L. Schuman, *Soviet Politics at Home and Abroad* (New York, 1948), p. 388.

[24] Erich von Ludendorff, *Ludendorff's Own Story—August 1914– November 1918: The Great War from the Siege of Liege to the Signing of the Armistice as viewed from the Grand Headquarters of the German Army* (New York, 1919), II, 263–264; *A King's Story: The Memoirs of the Duke of Windsor* (New York, 1951), p. 270; Arvi Korhonen, *Barbarossasuunnitelma ja Suomi—jatkosodan synty* (Porvoo: Werner Söderström Osakeyhtiö, 1961), pp. 90–91; Meiksins, *The Baltic Riddle*, pp. 137, 144; Josef Egmond Gellermann, "Mannerheim," in his *Generals as Statesmen* (New York, 1959), pp. 35, 40, 55, 150.

[25] C. Jay Smith, Jr., *Finland and the Russian Revolution, 1917–1922* (Athens, 1958), pp. 30, 219, 221, 223, 225, 227, 232.

[26] *Webster's Biographical Dictionary* (first ed.), p. 963.

The easiest, and at first glance the most reasonable, resolution to the conflicting interpretations of Mannerheim's politics is to conclude that (for instance in 1918) he "was neither pro-German nor pro-Entente. He was simply pro-Finnish."[27] This would be, for most Finnish political figures, a correct resolution. For Mannerheim, however, this is an overly simple and misleading interpretation. He was an extremely complicated, sophisticated, and atypical Finn; this fact, rather than lack of intelligence on the part of foreign observers, is responsible for much of the existing confusion about Mannerheim's politics.[28] It is remarkable that Mannerheim was not a Finnish nationalist. The Finnish nation, in his evaluation, was not the highest value. In 1922 he privately warned the King of Sweden that his fellow Finns were conceited and that their promises should not be trusted.[29] This view is hardly surprising when one remembers that at sixteen Mannerheim wrote: "I look forward happily to that moment when I can turn my back forever on Finland and leave—God knows where, but at least I can be my own master."[30] His relatives were justifiably worried that the young Mannerheim was becoming alienated from Finland.[31]

The crucial aspect of Finnish nationalism in the nineteenth century (when Mannerheim was maturing intellectually) was acceptance of the language of the Finnish-speaking majority rather than the language of the Swedish-speaking minority. Not only was Mannerheim born into a Swedish-speaking family, but he did not learn Finnish until

[27] George F. Kennan, *Soviet-American Relations, 1917–1920: The Decision to Intervene* (Princeton, 1958), p. 40. A less sophisticated variation on this theme is the observation that Mannerheim was "one hundred per cent Finnish." Austin Goodrich, *Study in Sisu* (New York, 1960), p. 29.
[28] Anthony F. Upton, *Finland in Crisis 1940–1941: A study in small-power politics* (Ithaca, 1965), p. 37.
[29] Heinrichs, *Mannerheim*, II, 468.
[30] Jägerskiöld, *Nuori Mannerheim*, p. 77.
[31] *Ibid.*, pp. 88, 261–263.

he was fifty.[32] He learned, and found much more use for, the great cultural languages of Europe before he mastered Finnish. A Frenchman who met him after the Second World War observed that Mannerheim spoke that precise French which one heard only from persons who had once been at the court of the Russian Emperor.[33] As Commander-in-Chief of the Civil Guards in 1918 he needed an interpreter to deal with his troops, as he did not yet know the language which most of them spoke.[34] Several delegations visited the Cabinet, demanding his removal as Commander-in-Chief because of inability to speak Finnish adequately.[35] As Regent of Finland, Mannerheim was not proficient in Finnish.[36] This linguistic deficiency was one of the factors

[32] It is mistaken, although politically useful, to assert that Mannerheim "had always known Finnish," as does Borenius, *Field-Marshal Mannerheim*, p. 128. It is equally incorrect, and much less politic, to assert: "In a household that spoke only Swedish, he didn't learn Finnish till the 1917 revolution, but now speaks that weird language perfectly." H. B. Elliston, *Finland Fights* (Boston, 1940), p. 75. Gustaf Mannerheim's linguistically gifted sister, Sophie Mannerheim, who (unlike her brother) spent most of her life in Finland, never mastered the Finnish language. Tyyni Tuulio, *Vapaaherratar Sophie Mannerheim—ihminen ja elämäntyö* (Porvoo: Werner Söderström Osakeyhtiö, 1958), pp. 315–316.
[33] Heinrichs, *Mannerheim*, II, 50.
[34] Martti Pihkala to author, May 14, 1956; Blücher, *Suomen kohtalonaikoja*, p. 239; Heinrichs, *Mannerheim*, I, 100; A. E. Martola, "Marsalkka Mannerheim ja vapaaehtoinen puolustustyö," in Suomen Aatelisliitto, *Suomen Marsalkka*, p. 106; S. A. Harima, *Myötä-ja vastatuulta* (Porvoo: Werner Söderström Osakeyhtiö, 1957), p. 101; Matti Kurjensaari, *Jäähyväiset 50-luvulle* (Helsinki: Kustannusosakeyhtiö Tammi, 1960), p. 69; Artturi Leinonen, *Kahden lipun alla—Romaani* (Porvoo: Werner Söderström Osakeyhtiö, 1953), pp. 146–147; *Presidenttikaskut—Kaskuja ja tarinoita tasavallan kahdeksasta päämiehestä* (Tampere: Kustannus Oy Lehmus, 1961), p. 78; Edwin Linkomies, "C. G. Mannerheim," *Oma Maa* (1959), VI, p. 48; Edwin Linkomies, "Mannerheim valtiomiehenä, in his *Ihmishengen tie—Valikoima puheita* (Helsinki: Kustannusosakeyhtiö Otava, 1954), p. 175; Eino Jutikkala and Kauko Pirinen, *A History of Finland* (translated by Paul Sjöblom, New York, 1962), p. 255.
[35] Heinrichs, *Mannerheim*, I, 101.
[36] Enckell, *Poliittiset Muistelmani*, II, 335; Enckell, "Muutama muistelma," p. 40; Paavo Virkkunen, *Itsenäisen Suomen alkuvuosikymmeniltä—elettyä ja ajateltua* (Helsinki: Kustannusosakeyhtiö Otava, 1954), p. 22; *Presidenttikaskut*, p. 78.

Mannerheim

Tanner

leading the Agrarian Party to oppose his election to the presidency in 1919.[37] To the end of his life Mannerheim's Finnish remained imperfect.[38] Before 1918 Mannerheim was unknown in Finland, except among his Swedish-speaking noble relatives and friends.[39] A member of the (conservative) Old Finnish parliamentary bloc later described a meeting of that bloc as the Finnish Civil War was beginning, on January 28, 1918: "Who was Mannerheim? Not one member of the parliamentary bloc

[37] Paavo Hirvikallio, *Tasavallan presidentin vaalit Suomesa 1919–1950* (Helsinki: Werner Söderström Osakeyhtiö, 1958), p. 11.

[38] *Presidenttikaskut*, pp. 79–80, 83–85; Lyyli Hagan, "Ihailin hänen henkistä ryhtiään," *Viikko Sanomat*, June 2, 1967, p. 31; Toivo Heikkilä, *Paasikivi peräsimessä—Pääministerin sihteerin muistelmat 1944–1948* (Helsinki: Kustannusosakeyhtiö Otava, 1965), p. 135; Jägerskiöld, *Nuori Mannerheim*, pp. 106, 108–110; Kalle Lehmus, *Tuntematon Mannerheim—Katkelmia sodan ja politiikan poluilta* (Helsinki: Weilin & Goos, 1967), pp. 231, 236; Linkomies, "C. G. Mannerheim," p. 45; Upton, *Finland in Crisis*, p. 37. Any doubt there may have been on this matter is completely removed by the release (by Otava) of two long-playing recordings of Mannerheim's speeches in a series, "Finland's Presidents Speak." To put it bluntly, Mannerheim's recorded Finnish pronunciation is beyond belief, ranking with Winston Churchill's French. Churchill, at least, did not have to govern the French. Perhaps the most confused comment ever made about Mannerheim's Finnish was: "There is a tradition that his Finnish was indifferent, but he never had difficulty in making himself understood in his native tongue." Oliver Warner, *The Sea and the Sword: The Baltic 1630–1945* (New York, 1965), pp. 157–158. No one, of course, has ever disputed the excellence of Mannerheim's Swedish.

[39] Ehrnrooth, "Carl Gustaf Emil Mannerheim," p. 18; Enckell, "Muutama muistelma," pp. 33–34; Enckell, *Poliittiset Muistelmani*, II, 330, 346; Voipio, *Suomen Marsalkka*, pp. 384, 399; Heinrichs, *Mannerheim*, I, 391; Yrjö Niiniluoto, *Suuri rooli—Suomen marsalkan, vapaaheraa Carl Gustaf Emil Mannerheimin kirjallisen muotokuvan yritelmä* (Helsinki: Kustannusosakeyhtiö Otava, 1962), p. 20; Heikki Renvall, in *Uusi Suomi*, January 28, 1951; Heikki Renvall, in Hildén, Numelin, and Fagerström (editors), *Sotamarsalkka*, p. 31; Onni Talas, *Ei se niin tapahtunut—vastaus Väinö Tannerille* (Hämeenlinna: Arvi A. Karisto Osakeyhtiö, 1949), p. 66; Kustaa Vilkuna (editor), *Maan puolesta—Urho Kekkosen puheita ja kirjoituksia 1938–1955* (Helsinki: Kustannusosakeyhtiö Otava, 1955), p. 267; Leinonen, *Kahden lipun alla*, p. 146; Erik Heinrichs, "Yrjö Niiniluoto ja Mannerheimin 'suuri rooli,'" *Helsingin Sanomat*, April 1, 1962; Johannes Virolainen, in *Helsingin Sanomat*, June 5, 1967; Niiniluoto, "Mannerheim: hahmo ja sen tulkinnat," p. 17; Upton, *Finland in Crisis*, p. 37; Jutikkala and Pirinen, *A History of Finland*, p. 255; "Myytti elää," *Suomen Kuvalehti*, May 27, 1967, p. 14.

could give an answer." [40] Four months later, Mannerheim left for Stockholm, having been ousted as Commander-in-Chief by the Finnish Cabinet: "My departure from Finland presented me with no difficulties, since I possessed neither a home nor goods. My earthly possessions could easily be contained in a couple of suitcases." [41] The reason for this rootlessness was that at the age of twenty, expelled from the Finnish Cadet Corps for disciplinary reasons, the young Mannerheim had decided to make his career in Russia rather than in Finland, as an officer in the Imperial Army. When, in December, 1917, after thirty years in that army, Mannerheim returned to Finland, he was, to use a formulation of one of his many biographers, "a stranger from a sunken world." [42]

The world of Gustaf Mannerheim was sunken in more than one respect: he was a cosmopolite in the age of nationalism; an aristocrat in the age of democracy; a conservative in the age of revolutions. These facts were at the same time his glory and his tragedy. That Mannerheim remained after 1917 an exception to the world about him was a measure of his individuality and personal integrity; his uniqueness, however, inevitably made him a leader without followers, a general without an army in politics. Mannerheim could not be a Finnish nationalist because of his language; he could not be an extremist member of the Swedish-language minority in Finland because of himself. After 1918 he resisted the efforts of these extremists to bring his famous name into their camp. Even though he was a Swedish-speaking Finn, it is not known whether he voted for candidates of the Swedish People's Party, to which a large part of the minority belonged. Furthermore, at a crucial point in the language

---

[40] Paavo Virkkunen, *Kahden sataluvun vaiheilta—elettyä ja ajateltua* (Helsinki: Kustannusosakeyhtiö Otava, 1953), p. 320.

[41] *The Memoirs of Marshal Mannerheim* (translated by Count Eric Lewenhaupt (New York, 1954), p. 184.

[42] Heinrichs, *Mannerheim*, I, 17.

struggle within Finland, in the 1930s, he publicly called for linguistic peace.[43]

In his personal life Mannerheim was conspicuous for the divergent nationalities of his friends and acquaintances. He had more personal friends outside of Finland than in it; within Finland his only close friend, outside the family circle, was Rudolf Walden, a wealthy industrialist.[44] Mannerheim's foreign friends ranged from Indian maharajahs with whom he went big-game hunting [45] to British and French aristocrats (notably absent were Germans). Before the First World War, while stationed in Warsaw, he found substantial personal satisfaction in the social life of the Polish nobility, especially as a member of the Cercle de Chasse.[46] While in St. Petersburg Mannerheim partook fully of the luxurious and cosmopolitan world of the Russian

[43] *Memoirs*, pp. 283–284; Voipio, *Suomen Marsalkka*, pp. 225–226; Heinrichs, *Mannerheim*, II, 60–62.

[44] G. A. Gripenberg, *Lontoo—Vatikaani—Tukholma: Suomalaisen diplomaatin muistelmia* (translated by Lauri Karén, Porvoo: Werner Söderström Osakeyhtiö, 1960), p. 346. Even this friendship was not as intimate as generally assumed. Lehmus, *Tuntematon Mannerheim*, pp. 221–222. A major theme of many students of leadership is the need for aloofness, for social distance between leaders and followers. Gustave Le Bon, *The Crowd: A Study of the Popular Mind* (New York, 1960), p. 140: Richard Schmidt, "Leadership," *Encyclopaedia of the Social Sciences*, IX (1933), 285; Ralph Waldo Emerson, *Representative Men: Seven Lectures* (Boston, 1876), p. 27; Kurjensaari, *Jäähyväiset*, p. 178. Of this social distance—mutually perceived—Mannerheim was an undisputed master. Kurjensaari, *Jäähyväiset*, pp. 73–74; *Presidenttikaskut*, p. 73. In view of his lack of followers, Mannerheim's aloofness approached political as well as personal loneliness. As someone who was relatively close to Mannerheim observed, however: "Eagles do not fly in flocks." Lehmus, *Tuntematon Mannerheim*, p. 241. This was already true of the young Mannerheim, as is movingly apparent from Jägerskiöld, *Nuori Mannerheim*, pp. 69, 239–240.

[45] "Where war and the big game hunt are absent, the charismatic chieftain—the 'war lord' as we wish to call him, in contrast to the chieftain of peace—is absent as well." H. H. Gerth and C. Wright Mills (editors), *From Max Weber: Essays in Sociology* (New York, 1958), p. 251.

[46] *Memoirs*, pp. 76–77; Ehrnrooth, "Carl Gustaf Emil Mannerheim," pp. 15–16; Rodzianko, *Mannerheim*, pp. 102–104; Borenius, *Field-Marshal Mannerheim*, p. 58; Heinrichs, *Mannerheim*, II, 14–15.

nobility.[47] He was a truly European *grand seigneur*.[48] For news of international politics—even during the darkest and busiest days of the Second World War—he faithfully consulted his favorite source of news, the *Journal de Genève*.[49] Mannerheim's last years were spent, appropriately enough, in Switzerland, where he was a man of the world to the end.[50] In his last years he remembered fondly his life in St. Petersburg.[51]

Such recollections were not accidental. Although he was a cosmopolite, he deeply and persistently loved the old Russia that he grew to know during his career in the Imperial Army. At the age of twenty he arrived in Russia, and was overwhelmed by the grandeur of it all. In the words of a sycophantic biographer: "And certainly, to a Finn, at the impressionable age of Gustaf Mannerheim in 1887, the whole was very strange, very wonderful: opening up, too, boundless fields for his ambition."[52] More than six decades later, the Marshal of Finland recalled this important decision: "I thus took a step which was to be of enormous importance for my future by removing me from the limited opportunities offered by my own country into a wider world."[53]

[47] Enckell, "Muutama muistelma," p. 34; Enckell, *Poliittiset Muistelmani*, II, 330.

[48] Jägerskiöld, *Nuori Mannerheim*, pp. 115, 230, 237; Erik Heinrichs, "Mannerheim ylipäällikkönä," in Suomen Aatelisliitto, *Suomen Marsalkka*, p. 57; Heinrichs, *Mannerheim*, II, 15, 406; *Uusi Suomi*, January 28, 1951; Blomstedt, "C. G. E. Mannerheim," p. 156; Heikki Kekoni, "Mannerheim yksityishenkilönä ja ihmisenä," in Karikoski, Kekoni, and Martola (editors), *C. G. Mannerheim*, p. 210; Niiniluoto, "Mannerheim: hahmo ja sen tulkinnat," p. 17.

[49] Heinrichs, *Mannerheim*, II, 188, 329, 420–421; Erik Heinrichs, "Kolmen sodan ylipäällikkö," *Uusi Suomi*, January 28, 1951.

[50] G. A. Gripenberg, "Marsakkla Mannerheimin luonnekuvan piirteitä," in Suomen Aatelisliitto, *Suomen Marsalkka*, p. 65; Raoul Palmgren, "Kansan ja herrojen presidentit, vahvat ja heikot presidentit," *Tilanne*, December, 1961, p. 58.

[51] Reinhold Svento, *Ystäväni Juho Kusti Paasikivi* (Porvoo: Werner Söderström Osakeyhtiö, 1960), p. 55.

[52] Borenius, *Field-Marshal Mannerheim*, p. 19.

[53] *Memoirs*, p. 5.

In this larger world Mannerheim married the daughter of a well-known and well-to-do Russian family; Anastasie Arapov's father was a general *à la Suite* of the Emperor.[54] This marriage could hardly have been perceived by the bridegroom as an act of national betrayal, for, as he wrote to his uncle in Finland, Russia was "our great Fatherland."[55] The Emperor sent his faithful Finnish follower on a major expedition to explore the Asiatic borderlands of his empire.[56] A Lutheran by birth, Mannerheim appears to have been overwhelmed by the Russian Orthodox Easter.[57] During the Second World War the Commander-in-Chief was angered by the plans of some Finns to send Lutheran missionaries to convert the (Orthodox) East Karelians.[58] Although he was never known as a practicing Christian, Mannerheim was buried with a gold cross, which he had long carried next to his heart, in the Orthodox fashion.[59] At the coronation of Emperor Nicholas II, he was one of two Chevalier Guards who, sword in hand, walked before the Emperor in the coronation procession.[60] Mannerheim, fifty-five years later, still remembered the ceremonies preceding the coronation as

[54] *Ibid.*, pp. 9–10; Borenius, *Field-Marshal Mannerheim*, pp. 20–21; Heinrichs, *Mannerheim*, I, 285; Rodzianko, *Mannerheim*, pp. 50–52. Gustaf and Anastasie Mannerheim separated after seven years of marriage, and were eventually divorced many years later. Heinrichs, *Mannerheim*, II, 40–41. After he had become famous, Mannerheim confessed that he had been a failure as a husband and father. Blomstedt, "C. G. E. Mannerheim," p. 147. As a father, Paasikivi was no better. Ida Pekari, "Lukulamppu, kävelykeppi, frakki—Hellsténin pojasta tasavallan päämieheksi," in Kauko Kare (editor), *J. K. Paasikivi: Itsenäisyyys—rauha—valtiollinen sivistys* (Hämeenlinna: Arvi A. Karisto Osakeyhtiö, 1960), pp. 130–131, 133.

[55] Jägerskiöld, *Nuori Mannerheim*, p. 105.

[56] The record of this trip was eventually published as C. G. Mannerheim, *Across Asia from West to East in 1906–1908* (two volumes, Helsinki: Suomalais-ugrilainen seura, Kansatieteellisiä julkaisuja, VIII, 1940).

[57] *Memoirs*, p. 10; Rodzianko, *Mannerheim*, pp. 30–31, 98.

[58] Gripenberg, *Lontoo*, pp. 241–242.

[59] Ehrnrooth, "Carl Gustaf Emil Mannerheim," p. 32; Niiniluoto, *Suuri rooli*, pp. 73–74.

[60] Borenius, *Field-Marshal Mannerheim*, p. 21; Rodzianko, *Mannerheim*, p. 54.

"indescribably magnificent." [61] He volunteered for service in the Russo-Japanese War, even though General Brusilov disapproved.[62] In that War Mannerheim served under General Kuropatkin, who in Finland was "particularly disliked as the chief instigator of the measure which led to the adoption of the Conscription Act of 1901 [drafting Finns into the Imperial Army] and to the destruction of the Finnish army." [63] At the same time that Gustaf Mannerheim was fighting in the Russo-Japanese War his brother Carl was in exile from Finland because of his opposition to Russification measures. Although Carl Mannerheim objected vigorously to his brother's participation in the war,[64] there is no sign that the latter suffered pangs of conscience at this (or any other) time concerning service in the Imperial Army. During the Russo-Japanese War, Finns who were working actively for Finnish independence not only hoped for a Russian defeat [65] but were able to purchase arms with Japanese funds.[66] Even those Finns who supported a relatively conciliatory attitude toward Russia viewed Russian military setbacks with satisfaction.[67]

In the First World War Mannerheim fought for Russia, rising to the rank of Lieutenant General, in command of the Sixth Cavalry Army Corps in Transylvania. Even after he

[61] *Memoirs*, p. 11.
[62] *Ibid.*, pp. 13–14; Rodzianko, *Mannerheim*, p. 61; Borenius, *Field-Marshal Mannerheim*, p. 32.
[63] Borenius, *Field-Marshal Mannerheim*, p. 32.
[64] Heinrichs, *Mannerheim*, II, 40; Niiniluoto, *Suuri rooli*, pp. 15–16; Jägerskiöld, *Nuori Mannerheim*, pp. 298, 301, 303–304, 380, 383.
[65] Herman Gummerus in Juhlatoimikunta (editors), *P. E. Svinhufvud 1861–1936* (Helsinki: Kustannusosakeyhtiö Otava, 1936), pp. 11, 15; Wihtori Kosola, *Viimeistä piirtoa myöten—muistelmia elämäni varrelta* (Lapua: Lapuan kirjapaino, 1935), p. 57.
[66] K. G. Idman, *Maame itsenäistymisen vuosilta—Muistelmia* (Porvoo: Werner Söderström Osakeyhtiö, 1953), p. 22; Kalle Väänänen, *Vainotien vartijat—Etelä-Karjalan maanpuolustushistoriaa* (Viipuri: Viipurin suojeluskuntapiirin piiriesikunta, 1939), p. 26.
[67] *Paasikiven muistelmia sortovuosilta*, I (Porvoo: Werner Söderström Osakeyhtiö, 1957), p. 136.

left Russia in 1917 Mannerheim felt a sense of loyalty and gratitude toward the Imperial Government which had been so generous to him for so long.[68] One of the less important —but revealing—ways in which this loyalty and gratitude was manifested were the regular visits paid to the Dowager Empress Maria Feodorovna in Denmark in the interwar years.[69] In his Helsinki home was displayed an autographed portrait of the last Emperor of Russia. When visitors expressed surprise at this fact, Mannerheim responded: "He was my Emperor."[70] The definitive statement of Mannerheim's attitude toward the old Russia was given when, near the end of his life, he remembered his return to Finland after the October Revolution:

> My thirty years of service in the Imperial Army were ended. It was with great expectations I had begun them in Russia, that vast and alien country, and when I now looked back on the many years I had worn the uniform of the Tsar, I had to admit with gratitude that my expectations had been fulfilled. I had entered into wider fields which had given me a broader vision than I could have had had I remained in Finland in the years around the turn of the century. I had been fortunate in belonging to, and in commanding, crack troops with good officers and excellent morale. It had given me great satisfaction to command troops such as these, both in peace and war. Also I had seen so much of great interest in two continents.[71]

After 1918 Mannerheim maintained friendly contact with his fellow officers in the Imperial Army.[72] They, in turn, remembered him with gratitude. In the early 1920s his former Commander-in-Chief, Grand Duke Nicholas, toasted

[68] Heinrichs, *Mannerheim*, I, 183–184.
[69] *Ibid.*, pp. 321–322; *Memoirs*, p. 9.
[70] Niiniluoto, *Suuri rooli*, p. 33.
[71] *Memoirs*, p. 124.
[72] Unto Parvilahti, *Berijan tarhat—Havaintoja ja muistikuvia Neuvostoliitosta vuosilta 1945–1954* (Helsinki: Kustannusosakeyhtiö Otava, 1958), pp. 97–98, 120.

him as a man who had fulfilled his obligations.[73] After Mannerheim's death former officers in the Imperial Army held a Requiem Mass in Paris for their former comrade-in-arms.[74]

One concrete reminder of Mannerheim's life in Russia during the three decades of his participation in Finnish politics was his ability to use the Russian language. This was an advantage which, remarkably enough, was shared by very few other Finns in public life, except for other members of the generation of older conservatives like J. K. Paasikivi. This linguistic talent was by no means the only remnant after 1917 of a career in Russia. In a much more fundamental sense, Mannerheim continued to speak the language of Russian politics even after the Bolsheviks came to power. During the Russian Civil War he actively supported armed Finnish participation in it. After the Bolsheviks were firmly entrenched in power, Mannerheim consistently supported a policy of Finnish conciliation toward what he considered either legitimate or unavoidable Russian demands. In other words, he was vigorously anti-Bolshevik but never anti-Russian. This fact would be difficult to overemphasize. Immediately after the February Revolution in Russia Mannerheim unsuccessfully attempted to arouse counterrevolutionary sentiment against the Provisional Government.[75] This revolution made a deep impression on him.[76] Indicative of his attitude toward the Kerensky regime was the feeling that "Russia's grave-digger [Kerensky] . . . contributed actively to the downfall of Russia." Mannerheim drew from the history of the Provisional Government the moral that

---

[73] Heinrichs, *Mannerheim*, II, 9–10.
[74] Voipio, *Suomen Marsalkka*, p. 405.
[75] *Memoirs*, p. 115.
[76] *The Memoirs of General Wrangel, The Last Commander-in-Chief of The Russian National Army* (translated by Sophie Goulston, London, 1929), p. 16.

"socialists are incapable of defending democracy."[77] He therefore sympathized with the Kornilov Rebellion. In view of this attitude, it is hardly surprising that he continued his counterrevolutionary conversations with other officers after the October Revolution.[78] In Mannerheim's view, it was the obligation of those Finns who had served in the Imperial Army to prevent a Bolshevik takeover of Finland.[79] Such a task, however, was much too small to satisfy his dream of personal grandeur. After his return to Finland Mannerheim saw as his life's mission the continuation of the struggle against Bolshevism,[80] which he considered the most barbarous of all despotisms,[81] a menace to the civilized world.[82] A close associate referred to Mannerheim as an apostle of anti-Communism.[83] Mannerheim wanted to lead Russia back to the old regime in a Crusade against Bolshevism.[84] He was not alone in this evaluation of his capabilities. No less a personage than Emperor William II considered Mannerheim to be the appropriate leader of the counterrevolution in Russia.[85]

For Mannerheim the Finish "War of Independence" was merely one aspect of military action on a broad scale to

[77] *Memoirs*, p. 128. The author of this statement today lies buried among some of his soldiers from the Second World War, almost half of whom were Marxists of one shade or another. The contrast between these soldiers and their Commander-in-Chief was, of course, as great as the contrast between two worlds, as has been observed by Matti Kurjensaari, *Jäähyväiset 50-luvulle* (Helsinki: Kustannusosakeyhtiö Tammi, 1960), p. 264.

[78] *Memoirs*, pp. 120, 122.

[79] Martin Wetzer, "Muuan kohtaus Karpaateilla," in Suomen Aatelisliitto, *Suomen Marsalkka*, p. 89.

[80] Enckell, "Muutama muistelma," p. 44; Enckell, *Poliittiset Muistelmani*, II, 338.

[81] Heinrichs, *Mannerheim*, I, 296, 378.

[82] *Memoirs*, pp. 197, 233.

[83] Heinrichs, *Mannerheim*, II, 51–52.

[84] Heinrichs, "Mannerheim ylipäällikkönä," p. 57; Heinrichs, *Mannerheim*, I, 356.

[85] Heinrichs, *Mannerheim*, I, 253; Yrjö Nurmio, *Suomen itsenäistyminen ja Saksa* (Porvoo: Werner Söderström Osakeyhtiö, 1957), pp. 215–219.

overthrow the Bolshevik Government in Russia. According to the German Minister in Finland, during this war Mannerheim tried to avoid anything which might make his loyalty to the old Russia appear questionable.[86] In a proclamation addressed to "Russia's brave soldiers" (that is, those Russian troops still in Finland), dated January 30, 1918, he stated: "Those under my command, the farmers' troops of the independent Republic of Finland, are not fighting against Russia, but have risen to defend freedom and the legal government, and to subdue without pity those groups of hooligans and bandits who publicly threaten the country's legal order as well as property."[87] Once Finland was rid of the Bolsheviks, the larger task could begin. After initiating the war in Finland, Mannerheim "sent information about the victory to Stockholm, from where the news spread over Europe. In the hope that the fight against Bolshevism which the improvised Finnish Army had begun would be regarded as a common cause by all responsible and thinking people in our part of the world, I ended my message with an appeal to all who

---

[86] Niiniluoto, *Suuri rooli*, p. 29.

[87] Erkki Räikkönen, *Svinhufvud ja itsenäisyyssenaatti—piirteitä P. E. Svinhufvudin ja hänen johtamansa senaatin toiminnasta ja vaiheista syksyllä 1917 ja keväällä 1918* (Helsinki: Kustannusosakeyhtiö Otava, 1935), p. 520; see also Heinrichs, *Mannerheim*, I, 98. Later, of course, bourgeois Finns came to view the Finnish Civil War as a War of Independence in which Finland defeated Russia. The inaccuracy of this assumption is treated at length in my study of *Three Generations: The Extreme Right Wing in Finnish Politics* (Bloomington, 1962). The bitterness with which both sides fought the Finnish Civil War is indicated by Mannerheim's Order-of-the-Day to his troops, dated March 14, 1918: "The hour has come, the hour for which the whole nation is waiting. Your starving and martyred brothers and sisters in southern Finland fix their last hope on you. The mutilated bodies of the murdered citizens and the ruins of the burnt-down villages call to heaven: vengeance upon the traitors. Break down all obstacles! Advance, White army of White Finland!" Borenius, *Field-Marshal Mannerheim*, p. 138. In eulogizing Mannerheim it was later nevertheless argued: "Every kind of hatred between soldiers fighting on opposite sides of the battlefield was inconceivable to him." E. Heinrichs, "Mannerheim. Muutamia mietteitä Marsalkan muiston aatepiirista," in *Peruskalliomme maanpuolustus* (Helsinki: Suomen Reserviupseeriliitto, 1951), p. 16.

were able and willing to do so to hasten to our help in the struggle which was not only for Finland alone."[88] During the war in Finland Mannerheim received arms and other assistance from Russian counterrevolutionaries in Petrograd.[89] As Commander-in-Chief of the Civil Guards, he probably envisaged military cooperation between his troops and the Entente to drive the Bolsheviks from power in Russia. Mannerheim expected a supply of arms from French depots at Murmansk.[90] His intention was to march with his troops to Petrograd which, in his judgment, could be captured rather easily.[91] Given this objective, occupation of East Karelia and seizure of the Murmansk railway would be necessary preliminaries to the capture of the womb of the revolution.[92] During the spring of 1918 Mannerheim overcame his antipathy for Germans long enough to urge the German Minister in Finland to support German participation in the restoration of the old Russia.[93] As the war within Finland was drawing to a successful close, Mannerheim wanted to continue the war into Russia.[94]

Mannerheim's large policy was destined to remain largely

[88] *Memoirs*, p. 143. This appeal did not go unheeded. The response was particularly favorable among the Swedish extreme right wing. Many able Swedish officers joined Mannerheim's staff, enhancing considerably its military competence. Aid from Sweden was not confined to volunteers, however. "In this connection should be mentioned the great financial support given by Baron J. Mannerheim and Baron Karl Langenskjöld." J. O. Hannula, *Finland's War of Independence* (London, 1939), pp. 113–114.

[89] *Memoirs*, p. 132; Hannula, *Finland's War*, pp. 100, 110.

[90] *Memoirs*, pp. 123–124, 135; Carl Enckell, *Poliittiset Muistelmani*, I (translated by Heikki Impola, Porvoo: Werner Söderström Osakeyhtiö, 1956), p. 253.

[91] Borenius, *Field-Marshal Mannerheim*, p. 184; A. R. Cederberg, *Suomen uusinta historiaa 1898–1942* (Porvoo: Werner Söderström Osakeyhtiö, 1943), p. 180.

[92] "The Memoirs and Recollections of Rudolf Holsti: An Abridgement" (MS, 1930), p. 16, cited by Malbone W. Graham, *The Diplomatic Recognition of the Border States: Part I, Finland* (Berkeley, 1935), p. 185.

[93] Nurmio, *Suomen itsenäistyminen*, p. 219; Juhani Paasivirta, *Suomi vuonna 1918* (Porvoo: Werner Söderström Osakeyhtiö, 1957), p. 242.

[94] Heinrichs, *Mannerheim*, I, 222–223, 237.

unfulfilled. After the signing of the Treaty of Brest-Litovsk on March 3, 1918, such an advance upon Petrograd by Finnish troops was incompatible with the desire of the German military command to prevent a recurrence of hostilities on the Eastern Front.[95] The Finnish Government, anticipating the victory of the Central Powers, refused to risk German displeasure, even though the prospect of Finnish territorial expansion into East Karelia was by no means unattractive. Mannerheim therefore resigned as Commander-in-Chief.[96] The German policy with respect to an advance upon Petrograd by Finnish troops received its clearest expression in the supplementary treaty between Russia and the Central Powers signed at Berlin on August 27, 1918. Article Five of that agreement read:

> Russia will at once employ all the means at her disposal to expel the Entente forces from North Russian territory in observance of her neutrality.
>
> Germany guarantees that during these operations there shall be no Finnish attack of any kind on Russian territory, particularly on St. Petersburg.[97]

According to the Finnish Foreign Minister, his government had not been consulted concerning this guarantee before the signing of the supplementary treaty.[98]

Even after the military collapse of Germany Mannerheim's large policy met with insurmountable obstacles. He was elected Regent of Finland to replace P. E. Svinhufvud when the need for a foreign-policy orientation based on cooperation with the Entente powers finally became apparent

[95] Nurmio, *Suomen itsenäistyminen*, pp. 209–210; Enckell, *Poliittiset Muistelmani*, II, 111; Otto Stenroth, *Puoli vuotta Suomen ensimmäisenä ulkoministerinä—tapahtumia ja muistelmia* (Helsinki: Kustannusosakeyhtiö Otava, 1931), p. 84.

[96] Heinrichs, *Mannerheim*, I, 238–239.

[97] This treaty is reproduced and translated in United States Department of State, *Texts of the Russian 'Peace'* (Washington, 1918), pp. 179–189.

[98] Stenroth, *Puoli vuotta*, p. 96.

to bourgeois party leaders in Finland—after the Armistice had already been signed. As Regent, Mannerheim engaged in extensive negotiations with counterrevolutionary Russian generals, who were finally prepared to act. These discussions did not result in official Finnish participation in a march upon Petrograd, for the White Russians repeatedly insisted that Finland was within the historic boundaries of the Russian Empire and thus refused to recognize Finnish independence.[99] The fact that the Finish extreme right wing not only insisted upon White Russian recognition of Finnish independence, but also anticipated acquisition of considerable areas which (unlike Finland) were an integral part of Russian territory substantially decreased the possibility that Mannerheim's large policy would be carried out. These difficulties did not cause Mannerheim to abandon hope, however. Throughout 1919 his thoughts constantly centered on the idea of intervention.[100] As Regent he not only permitted Finnish volunteers to fight the Bolsheviks in Estonia, but he dictated the choice of Major General Martin Wetzer as their commander.[101] Furthermore, Mannerheim instructed Wetzer as to the way in which these troops should be used.[102]

Most Finns were convinced during the Russian Civil War that any Russian government, Red or White, was dangerous. This belief was not shared by Mannerheim. As Regent he reasoned:

[99] Heinrichs, *Mannerheim*, I, 340, 354, 356; Enckell, *Poliittiset Muistelmani*, II, 112–132; *Memoirs*, pp. 192, 198, 208, 220–221; James Bunyan, *Intervention, Civil War, and Communism in Russia April–December 1918: Documents and Materials* (Baltimore, 1936), p. 341; Leonid I. Strakhovsky, *Intervention at Archangel: The Story of Allied Intervention and Russian Counter Revolution in North Russia 1918–1920* (Princeton, 1944), pp. 198–212.
[100] Heinrichs, *Mannerheim*, I, 371.
[101] Einar W. Juva, *Rudolf Walden 1878–1946* (Porvoo: Werner Söderström Osakeyhtiö, 1957), p. 164; Vilho Helanen, *Suomalaiset Viron vapaussodassa* (Helsinki: Kustannusosakeyhtiö Kirja, 1921), pp. 130–131.
[102] *Memoirs*, p. 207.

To have taken part in an operation which, so far as Finland was concerned, would be limited to co-operation in the capture of Petersburg [sic] and securing a sufficiently large basic area for a stable and healthy government, would represent such a valuable service to reconstituted Russia as to provide in all probability the most enduring basis for future friendly relations. It would indeed be a generous gesture for a neighbour who had lived until quite recently under Russian oppression to repay this with chivalrous assistance.[103]

On October 28, 1919, after his voluntary withdrawal from Finnish politics, Mannerheim sent from Paris an open letter to K. J. Ståhlberg, the new President of Finland, stressing the urgency of Finnish military participation in the capture of Petrograd.[104] To the end of his life Mannerheim remained convinced of the soundness of his large policy. On the thirtieth anniversary of the Armistice, in a letter to a former colleague, he praised President Truman for the latter's firm stand during the Berlin blockade, and expressed regret that not everyone had seen the Bolshevik threat early enough.[105] As Mannerheim later reminded his readers, "Europe and the whole world have had to pay a heavy price for allowing Bolshevism free play in 1919"[106]

Mannerheim's hatred of Bolshevism never led him to support a Finnish foreign policy rigorously antagonistic to Russian national interest. After he realized that Bolshevism was in Russia to stay, he urged Finnish party leaders to meet the Russians half-way in negotiations. During the diplomatic discussions which led to the Winter War, Mannerheim favored more concessions to Russia than the Finnish Government was willing to grant.[107] As Commander-in-Chief of

[103] *Ibid.*, p. 233.
[104] *Ibid.*, pp. 234–235; Heinrichs, *Mannerheim*, I, 378–379.
[105] Enckell, "Muutama muistelma," p. 46; Enckell, *Poliittiset Muistelmani*, II, 339.
[106] *Memoirs*, p. 236.
[107] *Ibid.*, pp. 300–303, 314–315; Heinrichs, *Mannerheim*, II, 90–91, 97–98, 184; J. K. Paasikivi, *Toimintani Moskovassa ja Suomessa 1939–41-I. Talvisota* (Porvoo: Werner Söderström Osakeyhtiö, 1958), pp. 2, 69, 100–

the Finnish Army during the Winter War he recognized that the eventual outcome of the war could only be a Finnish defeat, and therefore, against public opinion, urged a speedy peace.[108] In the Russo-Finnish War of 1941–1944 Mannerheim led Finnish troops into East Karelia. It is possible he considered that the only alternatives were German or Finnish occupation of East Karelia, and chose the latter. In any event, he expressed the view that permanent annexation of East Karelia by Finland was not in the national interest of the latter.[109] Indeed, his Chief of Staff concluded that Mannerheim not only opposed territorial expansion to the east, but favored, even during the war of 1941–1944 ceding at war's end territory on the Karelian Isthmus which had belonged to Finland before 1939.[110] Much earlier than most Finns Mannerheim realized that Germany would lose the war and that it was therefore imperative for Finland to remove itself from the war before the final military collapse of Germany.[111] As President he led Finland out of the war and into that remarkably successful adjustment of Finnish foreign policy which came to be known as the Paasikivi line.[112]

The politics of Gustaf Mannerheim were so different from the politics of most Finns in the twentieth century because he was one of the last great aristocrats in European politics. He was a baron,[113] and his father a count. Gustaf Manner-

102; J. K. Paasikivi, *Toimintani Moskovassa ja Suomessa 1939–41-II. Välirauhan aika* (Porvoo: Werner Söderström Osakeyhtiö, 1958), p. 80; Väinö Tanner, *Olin ulkoministerinä talvisodan aikana* (Helsinki: Kustannusosakeyhtiö Tammi, 1950), pp. 52–53, 86, 123.

[108] Paasikivi, *Toimintani*, I, 122, 161; Tanner, *Olin*, p. 368; Heinrichs, "Mannerheim," p. 13.

[109] Heinrichs, *Mannerheim*, II, 236, 276, 306–307.

[110] *Ibid.*, p. 251.

[111] *Ibid.*, pp. 336–337, 347–348; Väinö Tanner, *Suomen tie rauhaan 1943–44* (Helsinki: Kustannusosakeyhtiö Tammi, 1952), pp. 165, 328; Gripenberg, *Lontoo*, pp. 272–273.

[112] Heinrichs, *Mannerheim*, II, p. 465.

[113] In Ilmari Kianto's popular marching song, the Civil Guards in 1918 mistakenly referred to their Commander-in-Chief as a count. This was

heim did not grow up among the masses, but in a castle. He never learned, or needed to learn, to be thrifty as the bourgeoisie or the proletariat. Fame was for him a very sharp spur. His life's goal was far above the ordinary.[114] Mannerheim, to use Alexis de Tocqueville's formulation, was one of those men who had been shaped by the old order, and who, despite superficial alterations because of the march of events, never changed out of recognition. Mannerheim's bearing aroused respect for his person—if not agreement with politics—wherever he went.[115] His most emphatic criticism of others came when he felt that they had not acted in a chivalrous manner.[116] His personal experiences in the Russian Revolution reveal the kind of man he was. With many other representatives of the old Russia, Mannerheim spent the evening of March 11, 1917, at a ballet performance in the Imperial Opera. Upon emerging from this gala event, he encountered on the street for the first time the revolution.[117] When he finally decided to return to Finland, in December, 1917, Mannerheim refused to make any concessions to the fact that the equalitarian revolution was omnipresent and apparently omnipotent. He traveled from Odessa to Petrograd in a private railway car, dressed in the full uniform of an Imperial Corps Commander.[118] Upon arrival in Petrograd "it disgusted me to see generals carrying

merely one sign of the fact that Mannerheim was unknown in Finland before 1918.

[114] Heinrichs, *Mannerheim*, II, 462; Paavo Rintala, *Mummoni ja Mannerheim—romaani* (Helsinki: Kustannusosakeyhtiö Otava, 1960), pp. 28–30.

[115] King Edward VIII considered Mannerheim the most impressive figure among foreign dignitaries at the funeral of King George V. Heinrichs, *Mannerheim*, II, 49; Voipio, *Suomen Marsalkka*, p. 230.

[116] Gripenberg, "Marsalkka Mannerheimin luonnekuvan piirteitä," pp. 64–65.

[117] *Memoirs*, p. 110.

[118] Borenius, *Field-Marshal Mannerheim*, pp. 68–69; Rodzianko, *Mannerheim*, p. 118; Martin Franck, "Husaarin muistelmia kenraali Mannerheimista ensinnäisen maailmansodan ajoilta," in Suomen Aatelisliitto, *Suomen Marsalkka*, p. 98; Räikkönen, *Svinhufvud*, pp. 217–218.

Ståhlberg

Paasikivi

their own kit. However, I found two soldiers who quite willingly took charge of mine."[119] Within Finland Mannerheim's aristocratic manner was unique, according to the German Minister in Finland.[120] Mannerheim's table at military headquarters during the Second World War was known among his aides, with good reason, as "Mannerheim's court."[121] Late in life he was compared by a Frenchman to a member of the court at Versailles who had survived to the middle of the twentieth century.[122] A Swedish count who served under Mannerheim in 1918 and again in the Winter War referred to his Commander-in-Chief as "the last Knight of Europe."[123]

Mannerheim's political thought was as aristocratic as his personality.[124] He neither understood[125] nor accepted[126] democracy, but he was not totalitarian in his politics. Totalitarianism, while antidemocratic, recognizes the fact that democratic ideals exist and therefore attempts to integrate all of society by maintaining the fiction of popular consent. The postdemocratic nature of totalitarianism was, if anything, more foreign to the predemocratic politics of Mannerheim than democracy. He wanted to retreat to the titled world of St. Petersburg drawing rooms rather than to advance to the equalitarian world of the concentration camp and the permanent purge.[127] Some would call his politics

[119] *Memoirs,* p. 122.
[120] Blücher, *Suomen kohtalonaikoja,* p. 21.
[121] Stenvall, *Marski.*
[122] Heinrichs, *Mannerheim,* II, 450.
[123] Elliston, *Finland Fights,* pp. 89–90; see also Taru Stenvall, "Marsalkka Mannerheim sellaisena kuin minä hänet näin," *Suomen Kuvalehti,* May 27, 1967, p. 62; L. A. Puntila, *Suomen poliittinen historia 1809–1955* (Helsinki: Kustannusosakeyhtiö Otava, 1964), p. 122.
[124] Ehrnrooth, "Carl Gustaf Emil Mannerheim," p. 21.
[125] Blomstedt, "C. G. E. Mannerheim," p. 156; Kustaa Vilkuna, quoted in *Uusi Suomi,* October 16, 1962.
[126] Voipio, *Suomen Marsalkka,* p. 402.
[127] "He was an aristocrat, perhaps one of the last to rise to such a conspicuous place in world history. In the 'total world' it is no longer possible for the aristocrat to gain prominence in the practical aspect of society—and

reactionary, but at least he could claim with considerable justice that the new world was not even as good as—let alone better than—his world. Mannerheim never ceased to lament the arrival of democracy. In 1923 he complained that Poland, where he had spent such pleasant years before the Great War, now found it impossible to elect a suitably dignified head of state "because of democratic pressure." [128] He never accepted parliamentary government, the institutional expression of Finnish democracy. One of the major consequences of Finnish participation in the Revolution of 1905 was the abolition of the Diet composed of Four Estates, which was replaced by a unicameral Parliament elected by universal suffrage. Mannerheim described this truly radical reform almost a half-century later: "Were the Finnish people going to show themselves ready for such a revolutionary change? The answer was given eleven years later [in the Civil War of 1918]. It was in the negative." [129] It is difficult to imagine any other well-known Finn making such a statement—without being challenged.

In both 1918 [130] and 1919 [131] Mannerheim favored a monarchy in the struggle over the Finnish form of government. In mid-1918, however, he was in political exile from Finland, and his support for a Scandinavian [132] rather than a German prince as King of Finland was therefore politically

perhaps he does not even want to. The aristocrat cannot undertake to become an echo to the masses, and it is no longer possible to rise to power in any other way. The aristocrat could be in a conspicuous place today only as a dictator; it is impossible, in turn, to become a dictator without support from a party, whose formation would require wading in excessively muddy waters." Yrjö Kivimies (editor), *Suomen Marsalkka tuokiokuvina* (Helsinki: Kustannusosakeyhtiö Karhu, 1951), p. 6.

[128] Heinrichs, *Mannerheim*, II, 15.

[129] *Memoirs*, p. 24; see also Jägerskiöld, *Nuori Mannerheim*, p. 385.

[130] Borenius, *Field-Marshal Mannerheim*, p. 231; Heinrichs, *Mannerheim*, I, 235.

[131] *Memoirs*, p. 222.

[132] Idman, *Maamme*, p. 314; Anatole G. Mazour, *Finland between East and West* (Princeton, 1956), p. 59.

insignificant. By 1919, when he was Regent, monarchism was a lost cause in Finland. In 1930, Mannerheim supported the antiparliamentary Lapua Movement. Shortly before the crucial parliamentary election in October of that year, he issued a statement praising the "unselfish patriotic aims" [133] of this movement, which was outlawed in 1932 because its leaders attempted an armed revolt against the Finnish Government. Hindsight did not change Mannerheim's mind on this matter. He remained convinced that "this expression of the Finnish people's reaction to the abuse of freedom and democracy" had made possible an end to "the period of decay in the 1920s." [134] In his eyes the Lapua Movement was a demonstration of the fact that "even in the life of a nation, balance reasserts itself sooner or later, and the moment comes when the broad masses feel instinctively that order is preferable to unbridled liberty." [135] This Grand Inquisitorial conception of the relationship between liberty and order might have possessed some validity if the Lapua Movement had embodied order instead of anarchy.

Mannerheim attempted in 1940 to strip the Minister of Defense of some of the latter's powers in favor of himself (as Commander-in-Chief). The reason given by Mannerheim was that the Minister of Defense was responsible to Parliament, which in turn was subject to control by political parties.[136] In his attempt Mannerheim revealed the basic reason for his mistrust of parliamentary government. The idea of executive responsibility to an unrepresentative legislature would probably not have been repugnant to him. It was the fact that political parties—the people's great intermediaries, to use Sigmund Neumann's telling phrase—channeled both the election of members to a representative

[133] Heinrichs, *Mannerheim*, II, 19.
[134] *Memoirs*, p. 244.
[135] *Ibid.*, p. 243.
[136] Heinrichs, *Mannerheim*, II, 208–209.

Parliament and their behavior once elected which made parliamentary government so objectionable. Party activity was, in Mannerheim's judgment, symptomatic of an undisciplined, disruptive, and selfish attitude toward politics.[137] A leading Finnish political scientist has therefore concluded that Mannerheim was above parties.[138] This is true in the sense that Mannerheim refused to join or lead [139] any party. It might, however, be more accurate to say that Mannerheim was preparty (just as he was predemocratic) rather than above party in his politics. Rather than rising above political parties, he refused to acknowledge their existence. His leadership, when offered, was intensely personal. In a speech given in 1933, on the fifteenth anniversary of the end of the Finnish Civil War, Mannerheim made eminently clear his preparty conception of politics:

> Once upon a time, the sense of justice—enlightened and built up on time-honoured usage and noble traditions—was, especially for our people, more than the written law, the norm for the life of the nation and the actions of the individual. It was this sense of justice which shaped the personality, gave the character its strength, and brought forth resolution, the will to take risks and the readiness to bear responsibility. Nowadays, it seems to me, opinions are formed in quite a different fashion. It is far less the individual who, under the sense of profound responsibility, makes his decision; it is party opinion which—unhampered by traditional conceptions of honour—under the auspices of the vast agglomerations of people and split-up responsibilities, favours the commonplace, appeals to all that is undeveloped, and drastically hems in the intellectual mobility of the individual. Indeed, many indications suggest that the struggle and party strife of to-day are on the point of affecting

[137] Heinrichs, *Mannerheim*, I, 292.
[138] Göran von Bonsdorff, *Suomen poliittiset puolueet* (Helsinki: Kustannusosakeyhtiö Tammi, 1957), p. 64.
[139] It is confusing rather than clarifying to include Mannerheim in any classification of Finnish party leaders, as is done in Taylor Cole (editor), *European Political Systems* (second ed., New York, 1959), p. 765.

the very soul of the people. I hope, however, and believe, that if this is the case, it is yet something transitory.[140]

Unfortunately for Mannerheim's dreams of political leadership, the age of parties was not merely transitory in Finnish politics. In the twentieth century political isolation was the inevitable result for anyone who rejected party affiliation; party leadership and political leadership were synonymous. Mannerheim undoubtedly had real charisma, even though its extent was often exaggerated.[141] His career demonstrates, however, that charisma is no longer enough to ensure political leadership—if it ever was. If Mannerheim was cold toward Finnish parties, the latter were frigid in their attitude toward him. Finnish party leaders repeatedly made it evident that, in their judgment, Gustaf Mannerheim was by no means indispensable. The Finnish Cabinet was quite prepared during the Civil War to sacrifice his services as Commander-in-Chief of the Civil Guards in exchange for German military aid (which Mannerheim bitterly opposed). The Cabinet had gone so far as to find a ready and willing successor.[142] Mannerheim yielded. A short time later, in May, 1918, he resigned because of overwhelming opposition

[140] Borenius, *Field-Marshal Mannerheim*, pp. 248–249. An impressive example of Mannerheim's sense of personal honor is given by Heinrichs, *Mannerheim*, II, 326.
[141] Elliston, *Finland*, p. 74; Forbes, *These Men*, p. 281; Kivimies (editor), *Suomen*, p. 53; Niiniluoto, *Suuri rooli*, p. 77; Martti Simojoki, quoted in *Uusi Suomi*, January 29, 1961; Jägerskiöld, *Gustaf Mannerheim*, pp. 303–304; Kurjensaari, *Jäähyväiset*, p. 279; Stenvall, "Marsalkka Mannerheim," pp. 20, 62; Tauno Kuosa, "Mannerheim sotapäällikkönä," *Uusi Suomi*, June 3, 1962; Kuosa, "Mannerheimin sotapäällikkötaidon arvionnista," *Uusi Suomi*, September 30, 1962; Gripenberg, "Marsalkka," p. 69; Esteri Paalanen, *Uskon ja teon ihmisiä—Pienoiselämäkertoja koulunuorisoa varten* (Helsinki: Kustannusosakeyhtiö Otava, 1956), p. 54. Weber observed: "The charisma of the war lord may or may not be unstable in nature according to whether or not he proves himself and whether or not there is any need for a war lord. He becomes a permanent figure when warfare becomes a chronic state of affairs." Gerth and Mills (editors), *From Max Weber*, p. 252.
[142] Heinrichs, *Mannerheim*, I, 88.

to his large policy of Finnish intervention in Russia. Immediately after his resignation, "the members of the government had not a word to say to me when I left the chamber, and no one rose to offer his hand." [143] This coldness on the part of party leaders continued when, in 1919, Parliament elected K. J. Ståhlberg, instead of Mannerheim, first President of the Republic. After his overwhelming defeat in 1919 Mannerheim retired from public life. For the next twelve years he held no official position and was, politically, a very lonely man. The main reason for this isolation—symbolized by the defeat of 1919—was the rejection by the large majority of Finns of the idea of armed intervention in Russia.[144] This fact was expressed in direct language by a leading Social Democrat: "General Mannerheim was overthrown, I believe, by his stupid letter [to President Ståhlberg], in which he altogether incorrectly reviewed the prevailing policy and attempted to put poor Finland into the same state of bankruptcy with Mr. Yudenich." [145] Mannerheim himself recognized in late 1919 that his large policy had been doomed to failure because of lack of popular support in Finland.[146]

President Ståhlberg refused to appoint Mannerheim Commander of the Civil Guards even though the members of that military organization demanded the return of their war-

[143] *Memoirs,* pp. 182–183; see also Heinrichs, *Mannerheim,* I, 242–243. On January 20, 1946, Charles De Gaulle told his Cabinet he was withdrawing from politics. De Gaulle later described his departure from this meeting: "Not one of them said a word, either to ask me to reconsider my decision or even to say that he regretted it." Richard Harrity and Ralph G. Martin, *Man of Destiny: De Gaulle of France* (New York, 1961). Mannerheim's enforced return to Finland at the age of fifty has its analogy in De Gaulle's flight to the United Kingdom in 1940. De Gaulle described this experience: "At the age of forty-nine, I was entering upon adventure, like a man thrown by Fate outside of all terms of reference." *Ibid.*

[144] Heinrichs, *Mannerheim,* I, 392; Hirvikallio, *Tasavallan,* p. 12; L. A. Puntila, *K. J. Ståhlberg valtiomiehenä* (Helsinki, 1955), p. 2.

[145] Väinö Hakkila in Parliament, *Valtiopäivät 1921, Pöytäkirjat,* I, 364.

[146] Heinrichs, *Mannerheim,* I, 383.

GUSTAF MANNERHEIM 43

time leader and Mannerheim was willing.[147] The election of P. E. Svinhufvud to the presidency in 1931 gave Mannerheim an official post specially created for him: Chairman of the Defense Council. Mannerheim took this job seriously, and worked hard to improve the Finnish defense establishment. He met with considerable indifference from party leaders, even from conservatives whose campaign speeches were enthusiastically in favor of such improvement. J. K. Paasikivi, for instance, "as a former banker . . . was inclined to put other matters first and to cut down the appropriation for the armed forces."[148] Mannerheim decided to resign in 1937, since "my work has been thankless and the ideas I had initiated had not gained sufficient support from either the President or the government."[149] Only repeated urgings by Kyösti Kallio, the new President whose election intervened before Mannerheim could submit his resignation, persuaded the latter to stay on. In the spring of 1939 Mannerheim, as always, urged a conciliatory attitude toward Soviet demands upon Finland, but "met with no understanding."[150] Prime Minister A. K. Cajander was prepared, during the summer of the same year, to accept Mannerheim's resignation, and had begun the search for a new Chairman of the Defense Council.[151] During the crucial diplomatic negotiations in the autumn of 1939, leaders of the National Coalition Party privately criticized Mannerheim as too old and too afraid of the Soviet Union, and as—of all things—a man whose word could not be trusted.[152] Only a

[147] Virkkunen, *Itsenäisen*, p. 59. It is incorrect to refer to Mannerheim as "permanent Commander-in-Chief" of the Civil Guards, as does Forbes, *These Men*, p. 280.
[148] *Memoirs*, p. 270.
[149] *Ibid.*, p. 289.
[150] *Ibid.*, p. 300.
[151] Heinrichs, *Mannerheim*, II, 70–72; Vilho Tervasmäki, *Eduskuntaryhmät ja maanpuolustus valtiopäivillä 1917–1939* (Porvoo: Werner Söderström Osakeyhtiö, 1964), p. 37.
[152] Paasikivi, *Toimintani*, I, 75.

few days before the Winter War began, President Kallio, after much tergiversation, agreed in principle to Mannerheim's repeatedly threatened resignation.[153] If this plan had been carried out, and a new Chairman appointed, Mannerheim's retirement would probably have been final. The position which he held as Commander-in-Chief of the Finnish Army during the Winter War rested on the (secret) conditions of his appointment as Chairman of the Defense Council. Under the Finnish Constitution the President may in time of war delegate his powers as Commander-in-Chief. There is no reason to assume that the new Chairman of the Defense Council would not have been appointed Commander-in-Chief in the event of war. As it was, however, the Winter War began before Mannerheim's resignation was submitted formally, and, at the age of seventy-two, Mannerheim undertook the arduous task of leading the Finnish Army in two wars.[154]

[153] *Memoirs*, p. 319.

[154] It should be noted that Gustaf Mannerheim was never *in* the Finnish Army. He was, during the Civil War, Commander-in-Chief of the Civil Guards. The Finnish Army was at that time nonexistent, having been abolished by the Grand Duke of Finland (the Russian Emperor) during the period of Russification. Constitutionally, of course, Mannerheim's position in 1939–1944 was *above* the Finnish Army. He continued to serve as Commander-in-Chief throughout the uneasy peace of March, 1940–June, 1941. Paavo Kastari, *Tasavallan presidentin asema* (Porvoo: Werner Söderström Osakeyhtiö, 1961), p. 35; Antero Jyränki, "Yhdysvaltain ja Suomen presidentin aseman vertailua," *Politiikka*, 1962, p. 228; Antero Jyränki, *Sotavoiman Ylin Päällikkyys—Tutkimus tasavallan presidentille HM 30 §:n nojalla kuuluvasta toimivallasta ja sen käyttämisestä* (Vammala: Suomalainen Lakimiesyhdistya, 1967), p. 40; Aimo Pajunen, "Puolustuslaitos demokraattisen yhteiskunnan osana," *Politiikka*, 1965, p. 31; Upton, *Finland in Crisis*, p. 79; Risto Hyvärinen, "Foreign Policy Decision-Making and the Administration of Foreign Affairs," in *Finnish Foreign Policy: Studies in foreign politics* (Helsinki: Finnish Political Science Association, 1963), p. 106. Mannerheim was later criticized by the Speaker of the Finnish Parliament, Johannes Virolainen, for not yielding his position as Commander-in-Chief in with the resumption of peace in March, 1940. *Helsingin Sanomat*, June 5, 1967. There is no evidence to indicate that the Presidents of the Republic during this period—Kyösti Kallio and his successor, Risto Ryti—wanted to remove Mannerheim. Since, according to the Finnish Constitution, the President of

Mannerheim was elected President in August, 1944. There must have been moments, although they are unrecorded, when the new President felt some sense of compensation for his defeat in 1919. A quarter century earlier, however, he had been in the prime of life, prepared to do great things—especially in Russia. There was little that was triumphant about his election in 1944. Seventy-seven years old, tired, seriously ill, Mannerheim was faced with the agonizing task of leading a defeated nation out of war. The fact that the Finnish nation is today independent is at least partly due to his success in this task. The old unyielding physical strength and indomitable will were both gone, however. During the nineteen months of his presidency Mannerheim was frequently so ill that he was unable to perform his duties. Since these were no ordinary times in the life of the Finnish people, party leaders urged (politely but emphatically) that the President resign. The decisive request, to which Mannerheim agreed, came, ironically enough, from the Social Democratic Speaker of Parliament.[155]

Gustaf Mannerheim's career in Finnish politics, unlike his satisfying and successful career as an officer in the Imperial Army, had been one frustrating crisis of mutual confidence after another. All that remained were five quiet years, spent remembering the glories of a sunken world, and attempting in memoirs to convey the goodness of that world to future generations of Finns. That world had been generous to him,

the Republic may not delegate his position as Commander-in-Chief except in time of war, Mannerheim's position during this period was clearly unconstitutional. The final responsibility, equally clearly, rested with Kallio and Ryti. The standard introduction to the Finnish political system passes over the question of the legality of Mannerheim's position between March, 1940, and June, 1941. Jaakko Nousiainen, *Suomen poliittinen järjestelmä* (third ed., Porvoo: Werner Söderström Osakeyhtiö, 1967), p. 268. The Finnish "Who Was Who" states only that Mannerheim was Commander-in-Chief in 1939–1940 and 1941–1944. Iisakki Laati and others (editors), *Kuka kukin oli—henkilötietoja 1900-luvulla kuolleista julkisuuden suomalaisista* (Helsinki: Kustannusosakeyhtiö Otava, 1961), p. 329.

[155] Heinrichs, *Mannerheim*, II, 437; Hirvikallio, *Tasavallan*, pp. 137–138.

and Gustaf Mannerheim, being a noble man as well as a nobleman,[156] wished to express his gratitude appropriately.

Early on January 28, 1951, the Finnish people learned that the proud voice of the past was silenced. The older generations of Finns remembered January 28 well from 1918. On that date the Finnish Civil War had begun, and on that date Gustaf Mannerheim had first appeared on the stage of world history.[157] Everything about his life had been dramatic, and as a consummate actor Mannerheim would have appreciated the irony of the date of his death. The Marshal's baton was clutched firmly to the end by a hand which knew full well that "it is not as important for the potential leader to have been effective earlier as it is for him to be perceived to have been effective." [158] The myth around his name is perhaps adequate compensation for the essential failure of Mannerheim's life. It is nevertheless true that "the inspiring words and deeds of men who failed still live." [159]

[156] Paalanen, *Uskon*, p. 38.
[157] Heinrichs, *Mannerheim*, II, 459; Ehrnrooth, "Carl Gustaf Emil Mannerheim," p. 32.
[158] Bernard M. Bass, *Leadership, Psychology, and Organizational Behavior* (New York, 1960), p. 141.
[159] Herbert Hoover, *The Ordeal of Woodrow Wilson* (New York, 1958), p. 303.

## III

✯✯✯✯

## The Bureaucrat in Politics: Väinö Tanner

The late summer of 1914 demonstrated that for most European Social Democrats nationalism was far more powerful than Marxism when it came to a conflict between these ideologies.* Some Social Democratic parties did not participate in this demonstration, however. Not until the late autumn of 1939 did it become apparent that Finnish Social Democrats, for example, were nationalists before they were Marxists. The fact that Finland was not a belligerent in the First World War left this question open. Until the demands made by the Soviet Union in October–November, 1939, and the beginning of the Winter War (which included the abortive proclamation of a Soviet-sponsored Finnish Democratic Government), bourgeois Finns were uncertain about the response of Social Democrats to any serious Soviet challenge to continued Finnish independence. In view of the tragic Finnish Civil War of 1918, this uncertainty seemed grounded in historical fact. As the largest party in Finland (representing almost 40 percent of the electorate in 1939), the Social Democrats' attitude would prove decisive in determining the strength of Finnish resistance to Soviet diplomatic and military pressure. Like other Finns, Social Democrats fought, sacrificed, and died to defend their nation. The visible symbol of the unity of this nation in the Winter War

* An earlier version of this chapter appeared in *The American Slavic and East European Review*. Permission to draw upon that article is acknowledged.

was the Social Democratic Foreign Minister, Väinö Tanner. It was at this point that Tanner stepped into world politics. A Finnish scholar has stated that in the Moscow negotiations of 1939 the two Finnish delegates, Tanner and J. K. Paasikivi, "held the fate of Finland in their hands." [1]

The significance of Väinö Tanner in Finnish politics was more than merely symbolic, and of greater duration than a hundred days' war. For more than a quarter-century he was the most powerful Finnish Social Democrat. In times of internal and external struggle and in more tranquil times Tanner held a firm grip on his party. He therefore was probably the most powerful single leader in twentieth-century Finnish politics. Recognizing this, an American newspaper went so far as to state that Tanner "is to Finland's politics what Sibelius has been to Finland's music." [2] In 1943 the editor of Sweden's most important Social Democratic newspaper argued that "Finland and Tanner are one and the same." [3] Finns of several successive political generations would probably agree with this exaggerated evaluation in at least one respect: it is difficult to imagine Finnish politics without Väinö Tanner. Gustaf Mannerheim, who led bourgeois Finns in the Civil War of 1918, and whose general attitude was that "socialists are incapable of defending democracy," [4] nevertheless ended his life convinced that Tanner was a "great man." [5] Shortly before becoming President of the Republic in 1944, Mannerheim hoped that Tanner would become Prime Minister; even though this expectation was not fulfilled, Mannerheim still relied heavily on Tanner

[1] L. A. Puntila, *Väinö Tanner itsenäisyyden lujittajana ja puolustajana* (Helsinki: KKn kirjapaino, 1956), p. 11.

[2] "Stubborn Foe of Soviet: Väinö Alfred Tanner," *The New York Times*, April 18, 1960.

[3] Richard Lindström, quoted in *Sanat ja teot—sotasyylliset asiakirjojen valossa* (Helsinki: Suomen Kansan Demokraattinen Liitto, 1945), p. 24.

[4] *The Memoirs of Marshal Mannerheim* (translated by Eric Lewenhaupt, New York, 1954), p. 128.

[5] *Ibid.*, p. 271.

for political advice.[6] This favorable verdict of Tanner has been far from unanimous, especially among Finnish Communists. No less a personage than Otto Kuusinen publicly stated that Tanner was the devil in human form.[7] Communist newspapers in Finland labeled Tanner "Finland's Quisling"[8] and even questioned his sanity.[9] Yrjö Sirola, one of the most important emigrant leaders of Finnish Communism, considered Tanner a "thick-skinned hoodlum."[10]

Whatever one may think of Tanner as a person, one must agree with an American scholar that "it is, of course, impossible to deal with Finland's recent history without coming to grips with him."[11] To this one can add that it is impossible to understand the problem of leadership in European Social Democracy without coming to grips with men like Väinö Tanner. The crisis of Social Democracy is not only an ideological crisis, but a crisis of leadership as well. The transfor-

[6] Väinö Tanner, *Suomen tie rauhaan 1943–44* (Helsinki: Kustannusosakeyhtiö Tammi, 1952), pp. 338–339, 391–392, 395–396; Paavo Hirvikallio, *Tasavallan presidentin vaalit Suomessa 1919–1950* (Helsinki: Werner Söderström Osakeyhtiö, 158), p. 132. Tanner's attitude toward Mannerheim also underwent a radical transformation from open hostility to ardent admiration. Tanner, *Suomen tie*, p. 327; Tanner, *Kuinka se oikein tapahtui—Vuosi 1918 esivaiheineen ja jälkiselvittelyineen* (Helsinki: Kustannusosakeyhtiö Tammi, 1957), p. 346; Tanner, *Itsenäisen Suomen arkea—Valikoima puheita* (Helsinki: Kustannusosakeyhtiö Tammi, 1956), p. 272; Sir Walter Citrine, *My Finnish Diary* (Harmondsworth, 1940), p. 70; Anni Voipio, *Suomen Marsalkka—elämäkerta* (Porvoo: Werner Söderström Osakeyhtiö, 1953), pp. 241–242. In 1960 Tanner was among the few former prime ministers present at the unveiling of a statue of Mannerheim. *Helsingin Sanomat*, June 5, 1960.

[7] Yrjö Soini, *Kuin Pietari hiilivalkealla—Sotasyyllisyysasian vaiheet 1944 –49* (Helsinki: Kustannusosakeyhtiö Otava, 1956), p. 334; Arvo Tuominen, "Poliittinen vastustaja," in Olli Laitinen and Matti Nieminen (editors), *Kuin kallioon hakattu—Väinö Tanner 75 vuotta 12. 3. 1956* (Helsinki: Sosialistinen aikakauslehti, 1956), p. 128.

[8] Soini, *Kuin*, p. 232.

[9] *Ibid.*, p. 152.

[10] Tanner, *Kuinka*, p. 273.

[11] John I. Kolehmainen, in a review of Tanner's *Itsenäisen Suomen arkea*, in the *Journal of Central European Affairs*, XVIII (October, 1958), 352.

mation which has taken place within the *Weltanschauung* of rank-and-file Social Democrats throughout Europe is in a large measure an expression of changed attitudes among their leaders. Perhaps because recent Social Democratic leaders in many nations have lacked the colorful personalities of their predecessors—or perhaps because many students of politics are no longer interested in understanding individual leaders—relatively little scholarly attention has been paid to men like Tanner. Scientific generalizations must be the goal of the student of politics, but these generalizations are valid only so far as they are based on a knowledge of the political thought and action of individual human beings.

The political career of Väinö Tanner, like that of Ståhlberg and Paasikivi, was characterized by remarkable longevity. It spans almost the entire history of independent Finland and of the unicameral Parliament and universal suffrage. Tanner was elected to the first unicameral Parliament in 1907; he was last elected in 1958. Among the eighty Social Democrats elected to the first Parliament Tanner was one of eight twenty-six-year-olds; [12] in 1910, at twenty-nine, he became First Vice-Speaker of Parliament. In 1958 Tanner became the oldest member of an over-age parliamentary bloc. The youngest Social Democrat elected in 1958 was thirty-five, and only two others of the thirty-eight members of this bloc were born after 1918.[13] This aging of the Social Democratic leadership is both a symptom and a cause of the increasing difficulty which the Social Democratic Party is

[12] Other members of the first parliamentary bloc of the party who were born in 1881 included Matti Airola, Ivar Hörhammer, Kalle Hämäläinen, Alma Jokinen, Santeri Nuorteva, Armas Paasonen, and Sulo Wuolijoki. In the second election two other youthful Finns, destined to become world-famous, also born in 1881, were added to this bloc: Edvard Gylling and Otto Kuusinen. Väinö Tanner, *Nuorukainen etsii sijaansa yhteiskunnassa* (Helsinki: Kustannusosakeyhtiö Tammi, 1951), p. 318.

[13] Based on information obtained from official biographies of members of Parliament contained in *Suomen eduskunta 1958–61* (Helsinki: Valtioneuvoston kirjapaino, 1958).

encountering in integrating younger members of the working class into the party.[14]

Not only in Parliament were Tanner's services long-lasting. Throughout the period 1915–1946 he was Managing Director of Elanto, the immense consumers' cooperative in Helsinki. From 1927 to 1945 he served as President of the International Cooperative Alliance. Between 1919 and 1945 and again between 1951 and 1962 Tanner was a Parliamentary Trustee of the Bank of Finland. He first became Minister of Finance in 1917, returning to that post in 1937–1939 and 1942–1944; he was a Cabinet member several other times, including a year (1926/27) as Prime Minister. Even though his leadership was by this time purely nominal, his reelection as party leader in 1960 indicates Tanner's remarkable staying power. In all these posts the source of his strength was the same: Tanner was the first leading Social Democrat to gain power and prestige in Finland largely as a result of his administrative skills in the party organization, the cooperative movement, and the government. His ability to control a large bureaucracy distinguishes him from his predecessors in the party leadership. The first generation of Finnish Social Democratic leaders, men like Yrjö Mäkelin, Eetu Salin, N. R. af Ursin, A. B. Mäkelä, Matti Kurikka, Taavi Tainio, and Edvard Walpas-Hänninen, were primarily passionate publicists and orators.[15] These master propagandists, who resem-

[14] That its chief rival, the Finnish People's Democratic League (Communist), is having similar difficulties is argued in my article on "The Problem of Generations in Finnish Communism," *The American Slavic and East European Review*, XVII (April, 1958), 190–202. Of the fifty members elected on the Communist ticket in 1958, however, thirteen were born after 1918. In the 1962 election, four of thirty-eight Social Democrats and seven of forty-seven Communists elected were born after 1922. Furthermore, the youth activity of the Social Democratic Party suffers from the split within the party organization which began in the late 1950's, while the Communist youth groups are integrated and forever active.

[15] *Paasikiven muistelmia sortovuosilta*, I (Porvoo: Werner Söderström Osakeyhtiö, 1957), pp. 145, 182; *Paasikiven muistelmia sortovuosilta*, II (Porvoo: Werner Söderström Osakeyhtiö, 1957), pp. 4–5. Salin, who brought the young Tanner into the party leadership, did not want to run for

bled Keir Hardie in many respects, have been replaced by expert organizers like Väinö Leskinen, Olavi Lindblom, and Kaarlo Pitsinki.[16] For this new type of Finnish Social Democratic party leader Väinö Tanner was the model.[17] Tanner was not a demagogue [18] but at the same time he did not have the zeal and the vision that characterized earlier leaders of Finnish Social Democracy.[19] In 1925, when Tanner's type of leadership was still atypical of Finnish politics, one of his supporters wrote:

> ... in his earnest person there is not even the slightest sign of an orator. The sparkle of brilliant oratorical fireworks never lights up his speeches. No cheap phrase escapes his lips. He is matter-of-factness personified in everything that he speaks, writes, or does. He is above all a keen thinker and planner hardened in economic competition. It cannot be denied that in his entire intellectual essence there is something of the corporation tycoon—purposeful, sure of himself, and sharp, appearing correctly, with closed lips. He is thus a unique type among the leaders of the Social Democratic Party, but there can be no doubt that he is, precisely for that reason, valuable to the Social Democratic Party. This party—like all political parties—has enough persons who know how to make agitating

---

the first Parliament. After Salin had finally been persuaded to run for election, serving in Parliament "was for him like being in a penal institution. He was not made for parliamentary work." Tanner, *Nuorukainen*, p. 275. Walpas-Hänninen's desire to avoid the responsibility of taking part in party decisions is legendary among Finnish politicians.

[16] Matti Kurjensaari, *Jäähyväiset 50-luvulle* (Helsinki: Kustannusosakeyhtiö Tammi, 1960), pp. 43, 84, 250. This development has been part of the general decline in oratorical skills among Finnish politicians during this century. *Paasikiven muistelmia*, I, 204.

[17] *Ibid.*, p. 279; R. Palomeri [Raoul Palmgren], *30-luvun kuvat* (Helsinki: Kustannusosakeyhtiö Tammi, n. d.), p. 164.

[18] Yrjö Kallinen, "Johtajapersoonallisuus," in Untamo Utrio (editor), *Väinö Tanner 60 vuotta 12. 3. 1941* (Helsinki: Kulutusosuuskuntien Keskusliitto, 1941), p. 379.

[19] Pietari Salmenoja, "Taloudellisten asiain tuntija," in Utrio (editor), *Väinö Tanner*, p. 359.

speeches and to write fulminating articles, but who do not always have as many sharp leadership qualities.[20]

Careful planning in advance, equally careful devotion to detail in practice—these were the keys to political success for Tanner. Nothing was left to chance or improvization.[21] Since the Social Democratic Party was the first democratic party in Finland to achieve a high degree of organization,[22] Tanner served as a model for the entire Finnish party system.

There was little of the emotional or irrational about Tanner's behavior as a party leader. He seems far from charismatic leadership. Certainly Finnish voters did not decide to vote for or against the Social Democratic Party on the basis of their reaction to Tanner's personality. According to his own statements, he preferred cold calculation to emotion in politics.[23] He bitterly criticized party meetings which appealed to instinct rather than reason.[24] That Tanner's appeals to understanding rather than to passion were supported by so many Finnish workers for so long can only be considered a credit to these workers.[25] Tanner's dry, factual style of speaking [26] and writing has been sympathetically described as appealing more to older than to younger people.[27] Väinö Leskinen, typical of the bureaucratic or-

[20] Axel Ahlström, quoted by Aleksi Aaltonen, "Työväenjohtaja," in Utrio (editor), *Väinö Tanner*, p. 250.
[21] Untamo Utrio, "Miehen muotokuva," in Laitinen and Nieminen (editors), *Kuin kallioon*, p. 35.
[22] Jaakko Nousiainen, *Puolueet puntarissa* (Helsinki: Kirjayhtymä, 1959), p. 35; Martti Noponen and Pertti Pesonen, "The Legislative Career in Finland," in Erik Allardt and Yrjö Littunen (editors), *Cleavages, Ideologies and Party Systems: Contributions to Comparative Political Sociology* (Transactions of the Westermarck Society), X, p. 445.
[23] Tanner, *Itsenäisen*, pp. 76, 296.
[24] *Ibid.*, pp. 267–268.
[25] Kallinen, "Johtajapersoonallisuus," p. 379.
[26] S. A. Harima, *Myötä-ja vastatuulta* (Porvoo: Werner Söderström Osakeyhtiö, 1957), p. 214.
[27] Utrio, "Miehen muotokuva," p. 21.

ganizer in Finnish politics, has characterized his master's approach to party leadership as that of a businessman.[28] This is perhaps not surprising, since after graduation from secondary school (and before conversion to cooperation and Social Democracy) Tanner enrolled as a student in a business school. During the Winter War he impressed the visiting Chairman of the British Trades Union Congress as "a very solid matter-of-fact sort of fellow."[29] At the same time another sympathetic foreign observer concluded: "Tanner is a stocky little man who would probably pass in America as a fairly successful businessman in a small way. There is nothing distinguished in his appearance. He looks cold and precise and entirely unimaginative. It is when you see him chewing his cigar in ruminative mood that you think of the small-town American businessman pondering a proposition."[30] When first elected to Parliament Tanner chose assignment to the Finance Committee in preference to more exotic tasks.[31] Never did he have any use for what he considered the utopian bustle of most social reformers.[32] Least of all did he appreciate young intellectuals in his party. His contempt for the Academic Socialist Society, for instance, resembled the attitude of Martin Tranmael, leader of the Norwegian Labor Party, toward the *Mot-Dag* movement.[33] Rather, Tanner was, to use his own apt phrase, "a parliamentarian who stayed on terra firma."[34] He never attempted to

[28] Väinö Leskinen, "Puolueen johtaja," in Laitinen and Nieminen (editors), *Kuin kallioon*, p. 94. In an earlier parliamentary debate Tanner referred to himself as a businessman. *1932 Valtiopäivät, Pöytäkirjat*, I, 461.

[29] Citrine, *My Finnish Diary*, p. 63.

[30] H. B. Elliston, *Finland Fights* (Boston, 1940), p. 118; see also *ibid.*, p. 125; Hudson Strode, *Finland Forever* (new ed., New York, 1952), p. 204. That Tanner lacked imagination has been stressed by Kurjensaari, *Jäähyväiset*, p. 102.

[31] Tanner, *Nuorukainen*, p. 334.

[32] *Ibid.*, p. 192.

[33] David Rodnick, *The Norwegians: A Study in National Culture* (Washington, D.C., 1955), p. 141.

[34] *1931 Valtiopäivät, Pöytäkirjat*, I, 251.

The aged Mannerheim with his most faithful followers.

The aged Tanner—alone.

sketch the coming Socialist society.³⁵ For him Socialism as well as the cooperative movement was an instrument for concrete social and economic reforms rather than a goal in itself.³⁶ In his own view, he had no tendency to theorize; all abstract and philosophical notions were foreign to his nature.³⁷ In short, Tanner was a professional politician. Unlike many other Finns of his profession, he openly acknowledged this fact.³⁸

As a professional politician, Väinö Tanner found it necessary to take a stand on virtually every question of significance in twentieth-century Finnish politics. Any brief analysis is therefore bound to commit some injustice to the richness of his political thought and action. It seems justifiable, nevertheless, to seek understanding of his political thought and action in terms of his conception of the relationship between national consciousness and class consciousness. The struggle between these two allegiances has been the crucial element in the history of European Social Democracy, and it is this struggle which the student of comparative politics is obliged to observe. Tanner's approach to this struggle gave meaning and direction to his political career, and made him so intensely loved and hated by other Finns.

Tanner placed the Finnish nation far above the international working class in his personal scale of political values. This fact was of substantial significance for Finnish Social Democracy because of his power position. During the Winter War several of Tanner's friends jokingly referred to him as a "White." The instantaneous, sincere, and revealing response of the Foreign Minister was: "No, not white but

³⁵ Kallinen, "Johtajapersoonallisuus," p. 382.
³⁶ R. H. Oittinen, "Aatteen mies," in Laitinen and Nieminen (editors), *Kuin kallioon*, p. 81.
³⁷ Utrio, "Miehen muotokuva," pp. 17, 35; Tanner, *Nuorukainen*, pp. 21, 69; Tanner, *Näin Helsingin kasvavan* (Helsinki: Kustannusosokeyhtiö Tammi, 1949), p. 279.
³⁸ Tanner, *Nuorukainen*, p. 288.

*blue* and *white*."[39] Before the Winter War he had correctly predicted that if war came, the Finnish working class, contrary to bourgeois expectations (or at least arguments), would defend its fatherland.[40] After the Winter War he noted with pride that this prediction had proved correct.[41] Later, in the Second World War, Tanner stressed in a meeting of the Social Democratic Party leadership that the ultimate standard for judging all policy alternatives was the cause of continued national independence.[42] The importance of Finnish national independence in Tanner's politics was recognized by fellow Social Democrats [43] and scholars.[44]

Tanner was a nationalist but not an extremist. He differed from many bourgeois Finnish nationalists in that he did not desire to reduce the rights of the Swedish-speaking minority in Finland. Tanner, together with his party, recognized that Finnish should be the dominant language of Finnish politics, because more than nine-tenths of the population spoke it. At the same time, he considered it both possible and desirable to preserve the cultural autonomy of the minority.[45] In his nationalism he did not abandon the concept of class. He argued that Finnish-speaking and Swedish-speaking workers had more in common with each other than with the upper-class members of their language groups.[46] During a special session of Parliament held to consider the relation of Finnish-

[39] Citrine, *My Finnish Diary*, p. 59. Blue and white, of course, are the colors of the Finnish flag. Later, in his memoirs, Tanner related this story with obvious approval. Väinö Tanner, *Olin ulkoministerinä talvisodan aikana* (Helsinki: Kustannusosakeyhtiö Tammi, 1950), pp. 224–225.

[40] *1936 Valtiopäivät, Pöytäkirjat*, I, 852–853; Tanner, *Itsenäisen*, p. 212.

[41] Tanner, *Itsenäisen*, pp. 305–306.

[42] Tanner, *Suomen tie*, p. 236; see also *Helsingin Sanomat*, March 12, 1961.

[43] Oittinen, "Aatteen mies," p. 83.

[44] Puntila, *Väinö Tanner*.

[45] Tanner's conception of culture was clearly national in nature. Tanner, *Itsenäisen*, p. 119.

[46] *Ibid.*, pp. 198–199; *1935 Ylimääräiset Valtiopäivät, Pöytäkirjat*, pp. 57–58.

language to Swedish-language teaching at Helsinki University, Tanner created a political sensation by proclaiming that this was "a sixth-rate question" over which the working class could not get excited.[47] This characterization Tanner refused to withdraw.[48] In his judgment, social reform was far more pressing, far more important than the language question. The only reason that question was raised was to arouse the "primitive instincts" of the electorate.[49] The fact that the Social Democratic Party was partly dependent on the electoral support of Swedish-speaking workers no doubt contributed to Tanner's moderation on the language question. The caution of the professional politician was buttressed by the linguistic facts of Tanner's own background. As a child he spoke Finnish; he went to a Finnish-language secondary school, under whose influence he abandoned his Swedish family name, Thomasson.[50] His mother also spoke Finnish, but his father Swedish.[51]

Tanner was moderate in the language question because he realized that a Finland divided against itself on linguistic grounds would be weakened in its dealings with the Soviet Union. It was because he was so ardent a Finnish nationalist in his attitude toward Russia that he wished to avoid the language question in domestic politics. For Tanner nothing good had ever come out of Russia, except for the chaotic conditions of 1917, which made Finland's independence possible. He realized that Finland was part of Eastern Europe politically—that since the decline of Sweden as a great power the position of Finland in world politics depended

[47] *1935 Ylimääräiset Valtiopäivät, Pöytäkirjat*, p. 59; Tanner, *Itsenäisen*, p. 201. Tanner failed to see that any question which led to a special session of Parliament and immense public agitation was important. This was one of the few instances in Finnish domestic politics in which he confused what *was* with what *should have been.*
[48] Tanner, *Itsenäisen*, p. 261.
[49] *Ibid.*, p. 205; *1934 Valtiopäivät, Pöytäkirjat*, III, 3101; *1935 Ylimääräiset Valtiopäivät, Pöytäkirjat*, p. 61.
[50] Tanner, *Näin*, pp. 287–288.
[51] *Ibid.*, pp. 14, 41. 94, 134; Puntila, *Väinö Tanner*, pp. 4–5.

largely on Russian policy. In describing the crucial events of 1917 in Finland he recalled: "Everything depended on developments in Russia, just as so many times before." [52] The October Revolution "had, of course, a completely decisive influence on Finnish affairs as well." [53] Tanner recognized that because of its geographical position Finland had to live *next to* Russia; furthermore, Finland had to live *with* Russia. It was necessary to maintain good relations.[54]

Nevertheless, Tanner was unable to adjust his politics—as did Gustaf Mannerheim, J. K. Paasikivi, and Urho Kekkonen, for instance—to serve the end of good relations with Russia. Although Tanner was at home in several major European languages and nations,[55] he never fully mastered the Russian language.[56] This deficiency hindered him considerably in his negotiations with Stalin and Molotov in 1939.[57] Before that year, the only Russian city that Tanner had visited was Leningrad. He had not even been there for twenty-two years.[58] This was no accident. For Tanner Russia always remained "the unscrupulous enemy." [59] In a major speech in 1958 he warned that Finnish independence was in danger. The possibility that Finland might become a satellite could not be ignored. Russia, he said, always was a dangerous neighbor to Finland.[60] This statement touched off a bitter denunciation in the Soviet press.[61]

This speech, however much comment it aroused, merely

[52] Tanner, *Kuinka,* p. 42.
[53] *Ibid.,* p. 128; see also Tanner, *Itsenäisen,* p. 272.
[54] *1936 Valtiopäivät, Pöytäkirjat,* I, 854; Tanner, *Itsenäisen,* p. 214.
[55] It was in Germany that the young Tanner was first converted to Social Democracy; he remained loyal to his master Heinrich Kaufmann, until the latter's death. Tanner also maintained extremely close personal relations, not only with Social Democratic leaders throughout Western and Northern Europe, but also with cooperative leaders, especially in Scandinavia and Great Britain.
[56] Tanner, *Kuinka,* p. 53.
[57] Tanner, *Olin,* pp. 68–69, 183–184.
[58] *Ibid.,* pp. 61–62.
[59] Tanner, *Itsenäisen,* p. 304.
[60] *Suomen Sosialidemokraatti,* August 27, 1958.
[61] *Izvestia,* August 29, 1958.

reflected a lifetime of political opposition to Russian policy. This opposition began during Tanner's formative political years, which occurred during the period of intensive Russification measures in Finland from 1899 to 1914. His first political act was to sign the great address of the Finnish nation to the Russian Emperor, protesting Russification.[62] At that time Tanner was eighteen, just beginning to emerge from his apolitical home background to the larger world that awaited him. Further Russification measures aroused the same response in him.[63] Tanner's political generation, in contrast to other generations of Finns, had no experience during its formative years (approximately seventeen to twenty-five) of peaceful relations with Russia.[64] It was Tanner's generation of political leaders which was lost to Finland as a result of the war-responsibility trials after the Second World War.[65] All eight major leaders convicted at these trials belonged to the political generation formed by the period of intensive Russification. In view of the fact that their party affiliations ranged from Social Democratic to (conservative) National Coalitionist, the key to their strong anti-Russian views [66] was probably the anti-Russian milieu in which they experienced their formative years. All these convicted leaders were university students in their youth, and thus it is relatively easy to establish a date for the beginning of their formative years: the year in which they became university students.

[62] Tanner, *Näin*, p. 164.
[63] Tanner, *Nuorukainen*, p. 19.
[64] This point, as well as the significance of the concept of political generation, is amplified in my study of *Three Generations: The Extreme Right Wing in Finnish Politics* (Bloomington, 1962).
[65] The impact upon post-1944 Finnish politics of this loss was analyzed in an editorial in Finland's largest newspaper, dealing specifically with the problem of political generations. "Sukupolvien vaihdos," *Helsingin Sanomat*, December 16, 1956.
[66] That they were anti-Russian, of course, does not necessarily mean that they were responsible for Finland's participation in the Second World War. Their conviction was part of the price paid by the Finnish nation for continued independence of the Soviet Union. The price these men paid must be weighed against the price the Finnish nation would have paid if they had not been convicted.

Given the difference between Finnish secondary-school and university studies, Finnish family structure at the turn of the century, and the rise in social status which many of them—including Tanner—experienced when they became university students, this is much more than an arbitrary choice for the time at which they first began to think as individuals. The years in which they became university students were: Väinö Tanner, 1900; Henrik Ramsay, 1903; T. M. Kivimäki, 1905; Risto Ryti, 1906; T. H. Reinikka, 1908; Antti Kukkonen, 1910; Edwin Linkomies, 1911; J. W. Rangell, 1913.[67]

As so many others in his generation, Tanner opposed Russian policy even after Finland had gained its independence. The October Revolution failed to change his evaluation of Russia—it even strengthened his distrust of all things Russian. In the autumn of 1918 he anticipated the fall of the Bolshevik Government;[68] in 1935 he publicly hoped for democratic winds to blow over Russia—[69] he always looked forward to the collapse of the Soviet regime. In view of this attitude, it was hardly surprising that Tanner approved the hard policy of the Finnish Cabinet in resisting the demands of the Soviet Government in 1938 and early 1939.[70] It was even less surprising in view of the fact that Tanner was the most powerful member of the coalition Cabinet in power at the time. The Prime Minister, A. K. Cajander, was a member of the small and dwindling (liberal) Progressive Party, and did not even possess the united support of his own party.[71] In the autumn of 1939 Tanner felt that the chief demand of the Soviet Union, a lease to her of a naval base at Hanko, should

---

[67] These dates are taken from H. R. Söderström and J. O. Tallqvist (editors), *Vem och Vad? Biografisk handbok 1941* (Helsingfors: Holger Schildts Förlag, 1941).

[68] Tanner, *Kuinka*, p. 280.

[69] Tanner, *Itsenäisen*, p. 237.

[70] Tanner, *Olin*, p. 28.

[71] Tanner was correctly considered the "strong man" of the Cabinet, even by foreign observers. E. D. Simon, "Finland: A Democracy in the Making," in his *The Smaller Democracies* (London, 1939), p. 158.

not even be discussed.[72] Even after the hard policy of the Finnish Cabinet had failed to prevent war, he vigorously defended what he considered to have been the only possible policy.[73] During the Winter War Foreign Minister Tanner viewed Soviet military defeats as the precondition for peace negotiations.[74] Tanner's optimism concerning Finnish military successes led him to oppose J. K. Paasikivi's insistence on immediate concessions before the inevitable military defeat occurred.[75] Just as he had done in the autumn of 1939, Tanner held firm on Hanko in February, 1940.[76] This rigid opposition to Soviet policy aims continued throughout and after the Second World War. It was Tanner's policy before and during the Winter War, however, which met with the most serious criticism among his fellow Finns.

It is difficult for even a sympathetic observer to avoid the conclusion that before and during the Winter War the wisdom of Finnish foreign policy did not match the courage of the Finnish Army. Insofar as he influenced Finnish foreign policy during these months—and he did so decisively—the responsibility for this failure of foreign policy falls to Väinö Tanner. Part of this failure can be explained by his lifetime inability to grasp the essentials of foreign policy as well as those of domestic politics. His fellow Social Democrats [77] and Tanner himself acknowledge that foreign policy was his weak point.[78] The testimony of J. K. Paasikivi, Finland's greatest diplomat and his close personal friend, is significant in this matter.[79] In a radio speech to the American people

[72] Tanner, *Olin*, p. 54.
[73] *Ibid.*, p. 153; Tanner, *Itsenäisen*, p. 322.
[74] Tanner, *Olin*, p. 187.
[75] *Ibid.*, pp. 207, 270, 301–302.
[76] *Ibid.*, pp. 234, 248.
[77] C. O. Frietsch, *Suomen kohtalonvuodet* (Helsinki: Kustannusosakeyhtiö Tammi, 1945), pp. 99–100.
[78] Tanner, *Nuorukainen*, p. 213.
[79] J. K. Paasikivi, *Toimintani Moskovassa ja Suomessa 1939–1941–I. Talvisota* (Porvoo: Werner Söderström Osakeyhtiö, 1958), pp. 11, 13, 57, 64, 118, 134. For a fair, accurate, and negative evaluation of Tanner's gifts

during the Winter War Foreign Minister Tanner acknowledged that the uncertainties of international politics seemed strange to a realist like himself.[80] This was amply demonstrated when Tanner met Stalin in the crucial negotiations in the autumn of 1939. Tanner greeted the Soviet dictator with the proud confession: "I am a Menshevik." [81] It does not require much imagination to conceive of the impression this made on Stalin.

Soviet leaders, before and after Stalin's death, reciprocated this antagonism. In the view of the Soviet leaders and the Finnish Communist Party, Tanner was Public Enemy Number One in Finland.[82] Crude language and insulting invective attacking him flowed incessantly from the Soviet press and radio.[83] Tanner was forced to leave the Cabinet in

in foreign policy, see Anthony F. Upton, *Finland in Crisis 1940–1941: A study in small-power politics* (Ithaca, 1965), pp. 36–37, 56.

[80] Tanner, *Itsenäisen*, p. 296.

[81] Paasikivi, *Toimintani*, p. 64. A foreign publicist nevertheless wrote of the Russo-Finnish negotiations in the autumn of 1939: "Finland's Number 2 negotiator is ideally equipped, therefore, for international conferences. He has had the experience. He has the staying power. He has an uncanny knack of being right, which even his adversaries acknowledge—in time. And he is such a moderate in all things that the acceptance of his ideas and views seems to clothe any conference with the healing salve of compromise." Elliston, *Finland Fights*, p. 120. This judgment, at the very least, does not appear to have been supported by the actual course of events. Furthermore, it is based on a remarkable conception of the attributes of a successful diplomat.

[82] Tanner noted this fact, with apparent satisfaction, in his defense speech December 17, 1945, in his war-responsibility trial. *Väinö Tanner puolustautuu* (Tampere: Tampereen sosialidemokraattinen kunnallisjärjestö r.y., 1946), pp. 58–59.

[83] This fact led to the remarkable phenomenon in the postwar years, that Tanner the Social Democrat became the favorite of the Finnish right wing, especially the National Coalition Party. This affair reached its peak in the 1956 presidential election when he was the dark-horse candidate (although unused) of the National Coalitionists, but not of Social Democrats. A typical expression of this late-blooming love is given by Tuure Junnila, "30-luku minun näkökulmastani," in Toini Havu (editor), *Ilon ja aatteen vuodet* (Hämeenlinna: Arvi A. Karisto Osakeyhtiö, 1965), p. 131. Already during the interwar decades, Tanner was considered by the right wing one of the few Social Democrats worthy of personal respect. This feeling was articulated, for instance, even during the bitter 1931 presidential campaign.

August, 1940, when the Soviet Union stated that his resignation was the condition for amicable Soviet-Finnish relations.[84] Later in the same year Soviet leaders made it equally clear that Tanner's election to the vacant presidency would be interpreted to mean that Finland would not carry out the terms of the peace treaty of March, 1940.[85] During 1943 and 1944 Tanner's presence in the Cabinet was stated by the Soviet Union to be an obstacle to initiation of armistice negotiations.[86] The Soviet attack on Tanner continued even after 1944 for internal consumption within the Soviet Union.[87] It rose to a new pitch in 1957 when President Urho Kekkonen asked Tanner (however reluctantly) to form a new Cabinet.[88] The day after Tanner began this abortive attempt the Soviet Union announced that Soviet-Finnish commercial negotiations would be postponed indefinitely.[89] In 1959 Khrushchev took the occasion of the Finnish President's visit to Russia publicly to attack Tanner—in the presence of his visitor—as anti-Soviet.[90]

Soviet leaders had good reason to fear Tanner, for he never placed class above nation. His Marxism was moderate. In his own judgment he was always a revisionist.[91] Tanner saw Marx as a great scholar and founder of the international

"P. E. Svinhufvud presidentiksi," *Itsenäinen Suomi*, 1931 (Number 1), pp. 1–2.

[84] J. K. Paasikivi, *Toimintani Moskovassa ja Suomessa 1939–41—II. Välirauhan aika* (Porvoo: Werner Söderström Osakeyhtiö, 1958), pp. 66–70, 75–76; Lauri Hyvämäki, *Vaaran vuodet 1944–48* (Helsinki: Kustannusosakeyhtiö Otava, 1957), p. 27; L. A. Puntila, *Suomen poliittinen historia 1809–1955* (Helsinki: Kustannusosakeyhtiö Otava, 1964), p. 179.

[85] Paasikivi, *Toimintani*, II, 127; Hirvikallio, *Tasavallan*, pp. 89–90.

[86] Tanner, *Suomen tie*, pp. 145, 327; Arvi Korhonen, "Valtiomies," in Laitinen and Nieminen (editors), *Kuin kallioon*, p. 43.

[87] Unto Parvilahti, *Berijan tarhat—Havaintoja ja muistikuvia Neuvostoliitosta vuosilta 1945–54* (Helsinki: Kustannusosakeyhtiö Otava, 1958), p. 181; *Helsingin Sanomat*, March 12, 1961.

[88] *Uusi Suomi*, October 27, 1957.

[89] *The New York Times*, October 25, 1957.

[90] *Helsingin Sanomat*, January 25, 1959.

[91] Tanner, *Nuorukainen*, p. 316; Leskinen, "Puolueen johtaja," p. 95.

working-class movement; it would be wrong, however, to assume that the Social Democratic Party should hold fast to every detail of Marx's teaching; circumstances change from one decade to another, and someone who lived in the middle of the nineteenth century could not foresee the events a century later; the dead should not be able to determine the course of contemporary politics; every generation must understand and resolve its own problems. For this reason, in Tanner's view, it was just as wrong to call on Marx in day-to-day politics as to call on Snellman, the leading nineteenth-century Finnish nationalist.[92] Marxism had lost its justification when the first law for the protection of workers was enacted.[93]

The most important aspect of Tanner's rejection of Marxism was his acceptance of the goal of class peace rather than class struggle.[94] Unlike many other Finnish politicians, Tanner accepted the positive, British, rather than the negative, German, understanding of the concept of compromise. For him compromise was cooperative action toward a common goal rather than betrayal of one's principles. Constant compromise among the parliamentary parties was the natural order of things.[95] Throughout his long political career Tanner's words and actions reiterated his belief in parliamentary government.[96] The source of this attachment to parliamentary government, just as in his anti-Russian attitude, was the political climate of his formative years. The

[92] Tanner, *Itsenäisen*, p. 263; Oittinen, "Aatteen mies," pp. 79–80. Tanner's revisionism often revised not only Marx but the program of the Finnish Social Democratic Party. Tanner was capable of persuading his parliamentary bloc to ignore that program as out-of-date. Vilho Tervasmäki, *Eduskuntaryhmät ja maanpuolustus valtiopäivillä 1917–1939* (Porvoo: Werner Söderström Osakeyhtiö, 1964), p. 217.

[93] Tanner, *Itsenäisen*, p. 276.

[94] *Ibid.*, pp. 9, 209–210, 221, 240–241, 270.

[95] Tanner, *Kuinka*, p. 329.

[96] *Ibid.*, p. 82; Tanner, *Nuorukainen*, p. 351; Tanner, *Suomen tie*, p. 382; Tanner, *Itsenäisen*, p. 227; *1920 Valtiopäivät, Pöytäkirjat*, III, 2178.

unicameral Parliament and universal suffrage were the concrete embodiment of Finland's gains in its own General Strike of 1905, in opposition to Russification. Tanner's generation became the Finnish parliamentary generation *par excellence*. Its members, upon being elected to Parliament, made a life career of political leadership. During the interwar decades the composition of Parliament changed less after every election. Of two hundred members of Parliament elected in 1922, eighty-nine had never before been members.[97] Of those elected in 1930, fifty-two were new members, and of those elected in 1939, only thirty-four were new members.[98] It was this generation of leaders, committed both to parliamentary government and opposition to Russian policy, which was lost to Finland after 1944.

Considering Tanner's commitment to parliamentary government, it is not surprising that he refused to participate in, or even support, the abortive attempt of revolutionary Finnish Social Democrats to create a workers' republic in early 1918. Disgusted by the trend toward revolution within his party, he withdrew from active politics in late 1917. Tanner declined to be a candidate for Parliament. Indeed, for the only time in his life, he chose to stay away from the polls.[99] Nevertheless, he tried to use his personal influence to bring his party back to parliamentarism during the months preceding the Civil War.[100] Tanner was ignorant of Social Democratic plans to revolt in January, 1918.[101] After the Civil War began, he refused to become Minister of Finance in the

[97] Based on information obtained from official biographies of members of Parliament contained in *Suomen eduskunta 1922–24* (Helsinki: Kustannusosakeyhtiö Otava, 1923).
[98] Arvid Enckell, *Democratic Finland* (London, n. d.), p. 129.
[99] Tanner, *Kuinka*, p. 124; Leskinen, "Puolueen johtaja," p. 96.
[100] Tanner, *Kuinka*, p. 155; Leskinen, "Puolueen johtaja," pp. 96–97. Tanner was later severely critical of the evasion of responsibility by Oskari Tokoi, the Social Democratic Prime Minister in 1917. Tanner, *Kuinka*, p. 79.
[101] Tanner, *Kuinka*, p. 191.

revolutionary government.[102] Expecting the Civil Guards to defeat the Red Guards, Tanner stayed out of the limelight during the Civil War. Although he opposed the revolt, as a prudent man he kept quiet after it began.[103] All he did was to contact privately some of his more moderate bourgeois friends to investigate the possibility of an armistice.[104] Tanner's public silence was not broken until April, 1918, when he was one of the signers of a proclamation in a Social Democratic newspaper unsuccessfully urging an armistice.[105] By this time it was apparent to all that the Red Guards would be defeated. Tanner was already looking forward to the reconstruction of a parliamentarian Social Democratic Party in a bourgeois Finland. Undoubtedly he already then conceived of himself as the leader of such a reconstructed party, and this expectation encouraged his refusal to support the revolt.

As soon as German troops captured Helsinki in April, 1918, Tanner led a group of local Social Democrats who, like him, had not supported the revolt, in an attempt to revive party activity. This attempt was not immediately successful because of the repressive policy of the victorious bourgeois leadership. Tanner, for instance, was arrested three times for political offenses during the remainder of 1918.[106] In reviving his party on a parliamentary basis Tanner performed his greatest service to Finnish democracy. Together with K. J. Ståhlberg, the liberal first President (1919–1925) of the Republic, he was one of the two party leaders most responsi-

[102] *Ibid.*, p. 193; Leskinen, "Puolueen johtaja," p. 97.
[103] Tanner, *Kuinka*, p. 195. It is inaccurate to state that Tanner was "a reluctant supporter of the Red insurrection of 1918," as does C. Jay Smith, Jr., *Finland and the Russian Revolution 1917–22* (Athens, 1958), p. 90. The Communist interpretation of Tanner's attitude toward the Civil War is given by Antti Hyvönen, *Suomen vanhan työväenpuolueen historia* (Helsinki: Kansankulttuuri Oy, 1959), p. 333.
[104] Tanner, *Kuinka*, p. 200.
[105] *Työmies*, April 10, 1918.
[106] Tanner, *Kuinka*, p. 285.

ble for Finland's ability to maintain parliamentary democracy in a chaotic world.[107] This did not make Tanner popular with all Finns, however. The extreme right wing at first hated Tanner because it had expected Finnish workers not to recover politically from the disaster of 1918 for a long time—some estimated fifty years would pass before the working class would again be a significant political force. This hope was frustrated in 1919, when, under Tanner's skillful leadership, and with many Social Democrats still disenfranchised, the Social Democratic Party won eighty of two hundred seats in Parliament. The militant defeated hated Tanner because he completely disavowed the revolt. A major theme of his speeches and writings after 1918 was that the revolt had been a serious mistake. This judgment was expressed in clear and unmistakable terms, "cursing that absurd policy of adventure," which led to the Civil War.[108]

After 1918 the Finnish Communist Party became the spokesman of the militant defeated of 1918, especially the younger Red Guards. They worshipped at the shrine of 1918, which was for them the peak as well as the beginning of their political lives. Together with other Social Democratic leaders who experienced their formative years before 1918, Tanner wanted to forget the Civil War, which was a nightmare rather than a vision of tomorrow for him. Several decades later, he declared that one did not willingly remember the events of 1918.[109] Tanner repeatedly expressed the hope that 1918 would not need to be discussed in Parliament.[110] When this hope was not fulfilled, he attacked a

[107] Matti Leppo, "Valtiotalousmies," in Laitinen and Nieminen (editors), *Kuin kallioon*, p. 130. This fact was acknowledged in the remarkable autobiographical novel by one of Finland's few Communist literary figures, Raoul Palmgren. *30-luvun kuvat*, p. 84.
[108] Tanner, *Itsenäisen*, p. 10; see also *ibid.*, pp. 9, 13–14, 72–73, 271.
[109] Tanner, *Kuinka*, p. 194; Voipio, *Suomen*, p. 24.
[110] *1926 Valtiopäivät, Pöytäkirjat*, III, 3184; Tanner, *Itsenäisen*, p. 117; *1931 Valtiopäivät, Pöytäkirjat*, I, 265.

leader of the extreme right wing as a man who "does not remember anything but the events of 1918, he lives so far in the past." [111] Tanner proudly stated that Social Democratic activity did not aim to remind Finns of 1918, but to create a better future for the whole nation.[112]

It was in this attempt to create a better life for all Finns that Tanner encountered his most dangerous as well as his most determined domestic political enemy: the Finnish Communist Party. In 1919, shortly after the latter was organized, Tanner told a Social Democratic Party Congress that all Communists should be expelled from the party: "We must declare war against them." [113] Tanner fought hard, sometimes literally, against the younger generation of Finnish Communists, especially Arvo Tuominen, to prevent them from capturing the Social Democratic Party.[114] Tanner saw nothing positive in Communism,[115] and he had no confidence in former Communists, even when they repented.[116] In 1930, when they were effectively outlawed, he could not forgive Finnish Communists for having placed the interests of Bolshevik Russia above those of an independent Finland in 1918. Their "treasonous activity" had harmed every Finnish citizen.[117] In 1944, when the Finnish Communist Party was finally legalized, Tanner warned: "Its strategy and aims are poison to our nation, and we cannot even trust it to defend Finland's independence." [118] In his view, Communist activity had given birth to extreme right-wing movements in the interwar decades in Southern and

[111] *1935 Ylimääräiset Valtiopäivät, Pöytäkirjat*, p. 57; Tanner, *Itsenäisen*, p. 198.
[112] Tanner, *Itsenäisen*, p. 270.
[113] *Ibid.*, pp. 75–76; Leskinen, "Puolueen johtaja," p. 101.
[114] Tanner, *Kuinka*, pp. 302–303; Tuominen, "Poliittinen vastustaja," pp. 118–19.
[115] Tanner, *Itsenäisen*, pp. 95–96.
[116] Kurjensaari, *Jäähyväiset*, p. 102.
[117] Tanner, *Itenäisen*, p. 132.
[118] *Ibid.*, p. 347.

Central Europe as well as in Finland.[119] It was typical of Tanner's attitude toward the Finnish Communist Party that he privately urged conservative politicians to use all the force of the Finnish state, including the police establishment, against this party.[120] This advice was an expression of his belief that democracy could not afford to grant free expression to Communists and Fascists.[121] A democratic government threatened by shirt movements of one kind or another cannot receive them in its nightshirt, he said.[122] Whether such a policy toward mass movements can work seems doubtful. In 1937, seven years after the Finnish Communist Party had been outlawed, Tanner thought it had come to the end of the road.[123] Today, however, the Communist bloc is the third largest in the Finnish Parliament. Just as Tanner thought that Finnish Communism was a passing phenomenon, he thought that modern dictatorships were transitory.[124] When faced with lasting totalitarian movements and governments, Tanner did not know what to do. The achievement of Finnish independence and parliamentary government gave meaning to his political career, and he found it difficult to grasp the possibility that this achievement might not be permanent. Just as he could not believe

[119] Tanner, *Kuinka,* p. 338.
[120] Tanner, *Suomen tie,* pp. 370–371; Paasikivi, *Toimintani,* II, 76. Tanner illustrated well the truth of the observation: "A leader who has risen from the people is generally more authoritarian than one of aristocratic or middle-class origin." Maurice Duverger, *Political Parties: Their Organization and Activity in the Modern State* (translated by Barbara and Robert North, New York, 1963), p. 171. In this light one can understand, for instance, Tanner's strong support for the Cabinet of T. M. Kivimäki (1932–1936), whose enthusiasm for civil liberties of Finns was minimal. T. M. Kivimäki, *Suomalaisen poliittikon muistelmat* (Porvoo: Werner Söderström Osakeyhtiö, 1965), pp. 76, 86.
[121] *1931 Valtiopäivät, Pöytäkirjat,* II, 1927–28; *1932 Valtiopäivät, Pöytäkirjat,* I, 288; Tanner, *Itsenäisen,* pp. 187–188, 314.
[122] *1934 Valtiopäivät, Pöytäkirjat,* I, 857.
[123] Tanner, *Itsenäisen,* p. 267.
[124] *Ibid.,* p. 239.

that the human race would be so irrational as to engage in a Second World War,[125] he could not believe that an independent democratic Finland could disappear from the political map.[126] It remains to be seen whether his optimism concerning the future of Finnish politics was justified.

[125] Kalle Lehmus, *Tuntematon Mannerheim—Katkelmia sodan ja politiikan poluilta* (Helsinki: Weilin & Goos, 1967), pp. 14–15, 223.
[126] *Ibid.*, p. 224.

Ståhlberg, suddenly aged, after release by kidnappers, but with more followers.

The aged Paasikivi, triumphant, with Voroshilov in the flesh and another loyal friend in spirit.

# IV

✫✫✫✫

## The Scholar in Politics: K. J. Ståhlberg

In 1889 a young Professor of Political Science at Wesleyan University attempted to read the future of democracy throughout the world. Woodrow Wilson confidently assumed that all politics would be reduced to a single pure form. Democracy seemed about to prevail universally.[1] Thirty-four years later, in his last publication, Wilson, now a defeated statesman, sadly conceded that democracy had not yet made the world safe against irrational revolution.[2] It has become increasingly clear that popular government need not always be constructed along liberal lines. This is especially apparent in Europe, where liberalism, both as an ideology and as an organized political movement, has declined in support and vigor during the twentieth century. Mass support has been given to nonliberal and in many cases antiliberal movements. The response of liberalism to the challenge of these movements, as well as to the radical change in political environment that has come about during this century, has been pathetically weak. It has even been suggested that liberalism has committed suicide.[3] Whatever the accuracy of this charge, the kind of world envisioned by liberals be-

---

[1] *The State: Elements of Historical and Practical Politics: A Sketch of Institutional History and Administration* (Boston, 1893), p. 603.
[2] *The Messages and Papers of Woodrow Wilson* (New York, 1924), II, 1231.
[3] John H. Hallowell, *The Decline of Liberalism as an Ideology with Particular Reference to German Politico-Legal Thought* (Berkeley, 1943), pp. vii–viii.

fore 1914 has not, and may never, come into being. Concentration camps may well be the typical social institution of the twentieth century.[4] In such a world the liberal is naked and defenseless.

In Finland the decline of liberalism has been particularly marked. In the late nineteenth century liberalism was enthusiastically embraced by many younger Finns. During the period of Russification, which lasted intermittently from 1899 to the achievement of Finnish independence in 1917, liberals, organized as the Young Finnish Party, led the struggle to preserve Finnish autonomy. It was liberals, now organized as the National Progressive Party, who pushed through the republican constitution of 1919 against monarchist conservatives. The liberals then proceeded to elect their leader, the chief author of the new constitution, as first President of the Republic; the defeated candidate was Gustaf Mannerheim. During the first two decades of Finnish independence, the National Progressive Party played a crucial role in the formation of cabinets because of its central position in the multiparty constellation. It steadily lost popular support, however, to parties emphasizing the material welfare of a particular social class.[5] The Young Finnish Party had gained the support of 14.9 percent of the electorate (in the parliamentary election of 1911); the National Progressive Party support declined from 12 percent (in 1919) to 3.9 percent (in 1948). In 1951 the National Progressive Party was finally dissolved and the Finnish People's Party was formed, ostensibly in its place. The prolonged unwillingness to dissolve the National Progressive Party

[4] Max Beloff, *The Great Powers: Essays in Twentieth Century Politics* (London, 1959), p. 25.

[5] Göran von Bonsdorff, "Suomen puolue-olot," in *Tiedotuspäivät ulkomaille lähteville stipendiaateille ja asiantuntijoille* (Helsinki: Suomen Unescotoimikunta, 1958), pp. 31–32; Göran von Bonsdorff, "The Party Situation in Finland," in *Democracy in Finland: Studies in politics and government* (Helsinki: Finnish Political Science Association, 1960), p. 22.

organization, in spite of repeated electoral defeats, is a reflection of the stability of party structure in Finnish politics. This stability was not affected by the superficial rechristening of 1965, when the Finnish People's Party was renamed the Liberal People's Party.

Loss of popular support, by itself, need not signify the end of a liberal party. As Guido de Ruggiero has remarked, the strength of a liberal party does not consist in its numbers, but in its quality. The reconstitution of liberal parties depends on a recognition by the middle class of its integrating role in politics.[6] In this respect, the case of Finland is disappointing. Finnish liberalism has declined during the twentieth century, both in terms of popular support, and in terms of clear commitment to a set of principles. The opponents of the Young Finnish and (to a lesser degree) the National Progressive parties often argued that the liberal approach placed excessive emphasis upon constitutional principles at the expense of political realities.[7] The Finnish People's Party and its immediate successor, on the other hand, have played down ideology and stressed concrete benefits to small businessmen and white-collar workers, who formed the basis of their electoral support.[8] The Agrarian and Social Democratic parties always openly acknowledged their dependence on the support of interest groups, but the Young Finnish and National Progressive parties claimed to be

[6] *The History of European Liberalism* (translated by R. G. Collingwood, Boston, 1959), pp. 439–440.

[7] The criticism *par excellence* of the Young Finns' emphasis upon constitutionalism during the period of Russification is found in *Paasikiven muistelmia sortovuosilta*, I (Porvoo: Werner Söderström Osakeyhtiö, 1957); *Paasikiven muistelmia sortovuosilta*, II (Porvoo: Werner Söderström Osakeyhtiö, 1957).

[8] Göran von Bonsdorff, *Suomen poliittiset puolueet* (Helsinki: Kustannusosakeyhtiö Tammi, 1957), pp. 17–19; Jaakko Nousiainen, *Suomen poliittinen järjestelmä* (Porvoo: Werner Söderström Osakeyhtiö, 1959), p. 27; Jaakko Nousiainen, *Puolueet puntarissa* (Helsinki: Kirjayhtymä, 1959), pp. 15, 60–61; L. A. Puntila, "The Historical Basis of Political Life in Finland," in *Democracy in Finland*, p. 9.

based on ideology rather than class.⁹ A satirical novel about Finnish politics characterized the Finnish People's Party as willing to swallow its principles so long as the larger parties were willing to throw its members some crumbs from the common table.¹⁰ With considerable understatement, a Finnish political scientist concluded that its basic attitude toward other parties was ambiguous.¹¹

Above all, the decline of Finnish liberalism has been a decline of leadership. There are many able and competent persons in the Liberal People's Party leadership, but there is no outstanding figure to carry on the tradition of statesmanship established by Finnish liberals from Leo Mechelin to Heikki Ritavuori.¹² This lack was apparent already during the latter years of the National Progressive Party, when men like T. M. Kivimäki and Risto Ryti led the party—and sometimes the nation—in policies which could hardly be termed imaginative or successful.¹³ This bankruptcy of leadership is not confined to one party, but is especially apparent in a party whose earliest predecessors were characterized by an abundance of leaders. Liberals, therefore, exerted an influence far greater than their numerical significance would have justified. The predominance of distinguished jurists among earlier Finnish liberal leaders no doubt gave many

⁹ This dependence of political parties on interest groups is one of the major problems faced by Finnish politics. Lolo Krusius-Ahrenberg, "The Political Power of Economic and Labor-Market Organizations: A Dilemma of Finnish Democracy," in Henry W. Ehrmann (editor), *Interest Groups on Four Continents* (Pittsburgh, 1958), pp. 33–59.

¹⁰ Mauri Sariola, *Isänmaan parturit—romaani* (Jyväskylä: K. J. Gummerus Osakeyhtiö, 1959), p. 69. A variation on this theme is given by Pauli Burman and Matti Nieminen, *Osakeyhtiö Isänmaa* (Jyväskylä: K. J. Gummerus Osakeyhtiö, 1959), pp. 38–40, 108, 111, 138.

¹¹ Bonsdorff, *Suomen*, p. 56.

¹² Mechelin was the liberal leader during the Russification period; Ritavuori, an outstanding Cabinet member, and K. J. Ståhlberg's heir apparent, was assassinated by a member of the extreme right wing in 1922.

¹³ Kivimäki was Prime Minister from 1932 to 1936; Ryti was President of the Republic from 1940 to 1944. Both men were among those convicted in 1946 as "war responsibles."

nonliberals a sense of trust and confidence in the essential justice of liberal policies. Today, few Finns outside the Liberal People's Party pay deference to the interest-group spokesmen who lead that party. Fewer still would consider one of these spokesmen as "one of the great martyrs of the Finnish people"—a characterization of an earlier Finnish liberal, K. J. Ståhlberg, made by a distinguished literary figure.[14]

It may be questionable whether the object of such adulation was a martyr, but Ståhlberg was undoubtedly the most important, as well as the most interesting, Finnish liberal of the twentieth century. During the period of Russification, his intellectual ability gave direction to Finnish liberalism.[15] A future President of the Republic (not of his party) considered Ståhlberg the creator of Finnish parliamentarism.[16] Finnish scholars of divergent political viewpoints agree that Ståhlberg was one of the two or three greatest Finnish statesmen.[17] Even his enemies referred to him as the first citizen of the republic.[18] An impartial foreign observer concluded that no more able man could have been elected first President of the Republic in 1919.[19] Ståhlberg was "the great central figure" of the National Progressive

[14] Matti Kurjensaari, *Taistelu huomispäivästä—Isänmaan opissa 1918–1948* (Helsinki: Kustannusosakeyhtiö Tammi, 1948), p. 33. See also Matti Kurjensaari, *Jäähyväiset 50-luvulle* (Helsinki: Kustannusosakeyhtiö Tammi, 1960), p. 316; A. M. Tallgren, "K. J. Ståhlberg," in A. M. Tallgren, Göta Salovius-Sinervo, and Vihtori Laurila (editors), *Kaarlo Juho Ståhlberg—Juhlakirja 1940* (Helsinki: Aamun kannatusyhdistys r. y., 1940), pp. 12–13.

[15] Kustaa Vilkuna (editor), *Maan puolesta—Urho Kekkosen puheita ja kirjoituksia 1938–1955* (Helsinki: Kustannusosakeyhtiö Otava, 1955), p. 259.

[16] *Ibid.*, p. 260.

[17] L. A. Puntila, *K. J. Ståhlberg valtiomiehenä* (Helsinki: 1955), p. 13; Matti Leppo, "Valtiotalousmies," in Olli Laitinen and Matti Nieminen (editors), *Kuin kallioon hakattu—Väinö Tanner 75 vuotta 12.3.1956* (Helsinki: Sosialistinen aikakauslehti, 1956), p. 130.

[18] John H. Wuorinen, writing in *Current History*, XXXIII (December, 1930), 464.

[19] J. Hampden Jackson, *Finland* (New York, 1940), p. 110.

Party.[20] By the simplest of all standards, political longevity, his career was remarkable. Ståhlberg became a member of the bourgeois estate in 1904 and a Cabinet member in 1905, and as late as 1944 was offered the prime ministership, but declined for reasons of health.[21] In 1946, when he was eighty-one, fourteen members of Parliament voted for Ståhlberg to succeed Gustaf Mannerheim as President of the Republic.[22] In 1950, Ståhlberg was instrumental in the reelection of J. K. Paasikivi to the presidency.[23] Indicative of the longevity of both, as well as of the coincidence of their careers at many points in time, was the fact that Paasikivi succeeded Ståhlberg as Assistant Professor of Administrative Law at Helsinki University in 1902,[24] and that when Ståhlberg was named Professor of Administrative Law in 1908 one of those officially recommending his appointment was Paasikivi.[25]

The fundamental element of liberalism is a deep and unshakable faith in man's ability to shape his own destiny. This faith K. J. Ståhlberg possessed in abundant measure.[26] It was expressed, somewhat grandly, in his youth.[27] During some of the darkest moments in Finnish politics, when it seemed that none of the dreams of a liberal could be fulfilled, Ståhlberg simply but eloquently stated his faith in progress. In 1913, when Russification was pressed hardest,

[20] Bonsdorff, *Suomen*, p. 56.
[21] Puntila, *K. J. Ståhlberg*, p. 12.
[22] Lauri Hyvämäki, *Vaaran vuodet 1944–48* (Helsinki: Kustannusosakeyhtiö Otava, 1957), p. 102; Paavo Hirvikallio, *Tasavallan presidentin vaalit Suomessa 1919–1950* (Helsinki: Werner Söderström Oskeyhtiö, 1958), p. 141.
[23] Hirvikallio, *Tasavallan*, pp. 145–147.
[24] *Paasikiven muistelmia*, I, 134.
[25] *Paasikiven muistelmia*, II, 93.
[26] Vihtori Laurila, "K. J. Ståhlberg sanomalehdistössä vuosina 1890–1919 —Eräitä havaintoja ja reunahuomautuksia," in Tallgren, Salovius-Sinervo, and Laurila (editors), *Kaarlo Juho Ståhlberg*, p. 302; Hiski Mikkonen, "Ihminen, maailmankatsomus ja elämäntyö," in *ibid.*, p. 309.
[27] K. J. Ståhlberg, *Puheita 1927–1946* (Helsinki: Kustannusosakeyhtiö Otava, 1946), pp. 40–41.

he spoke, in language that might have been Woodrow Wilson's, of the universal advance of democracy.[28] Ståhlberg warned against false optimism, but argued that the precondition for political success—in this case, preservation of Finnish autonomy—was confidence that the goal could be reached.[29] During the interwar decades, when powerful forces in Finland were working toward totalitarianism, he expressed his confidence that the civil rights of Finns would not only be preserved but even expanded.[30] The defeat of parliamentary government by dictatorships in Eastern and Central Europe was, in his view, a pathological phenomenon which would prove transitory.[31] At his eightieth birthday celebration, in January, 1945, when a new and more dangerous Russification appeared imminent to many Finns, Ståhlberg made it clear that he expected Finnish independence to continue a reality.[32] This faith in the future was in distinct contrast to the pessimism of Finland's leading conservative, J. K. Paasikivi.

Ståhlberg was not alone in his optimism. In this respect

[28] K. J. Ståhlberg, *Puheita 1883–1918* (Helsinki: Kustannusosakeyhtiö Otava, 1951), pp. 144–145. It is worth noting that an important Finnish liberal identified Ståhlberg as the Finnish representative of the liberalism of Woodrow Wilson and Franklin D. Roosevelt. Arvo Inkilä, "Liberalismi," in Akateeminen Sos.-dem. Yhdistys, *Poliittiset aatteet* (Porvoo: Werner Söderström Osakeyhtiö, 1945), p. 108. There were other significant similarities between the careers of Wilson and Ståhlberg. Both were the sons of clergymen. Both were scholars whose approach to political analysis was largely institutional. One of Ståhlberg's admirers praised the object of his devotion as "puritanical." Tallgren, "K. J. Ståhlberg," p. 11. Most important, both Wilson and Ståhlberg were chief authors of constitutional documents in 1919. Ståhlberg's constitution lasted longer than Wilson's Covenant, however. The Finnish Constitution of 1919 is the only major document of that memorable year which remains a living force.
[29] Ståhlberg, *Puheita 1883–1918*, pp. 155–156; *Paasikiven muistelmia*, II, 130–131.
[30] Ståhlberg, *Puheita 1927–1946*, pp. 32–33.
[31] *Ibid.*, p. 124; *1931 Valtiopäivät, Pöytäkirjat*, II, 1140; K. J. Ståhlberg, *Parlamentarismi Suomen valtiosäännössä* (Helsinki: Kustannusosakeyhtiö Otava, 1927), pp. 87–88.
[32] Ståhlberg, *Puheita 1927–1946*, p. 77.

he was, and considered himself, a member of an entire generation of Finnish liberals who had been the first to be educated in Finnish-language secondary schools. In a speech to the youth organization of the National Progressive Party in 1945,[33] he defined the ideals of his generation: freedom under law without disorder, legal security which does not permit violation of the rights of others, democracy without defiance of legal forms and public order, and progress through constructive peaceful evolution rather than through destructive upheavals.[34] These had been the ideals of Ståhlberg's years as a university student.[35] The task of his generation of students had been to prepare itself to direct the destinies of the Finnish nation.[36] This task was completed, for Ståhlberg's generation witnessed the achievement and acceptance of Finnish independence.[37]

The crucial issue of Finnish politics during Ståhlberg's youth was the relationship of the Finnish and Swedish languages. He was one of the first students at Helsinki University to request—and receive—permission to use the Finnish language in examinations and papers.[38] Ståhlberg was a nationalist, and language was the most important element of nationality in his judgment.[39] Common experiences, institutions, and culture, together with a more developed consciousness, had made of a linguistic group something higher: the Finnish nation, with common joys and worries, common recollections and hopes for the future.[40] Hard work, rather than festive speeches, was the criterion of the strength of

[33] This speech has been characterized as presenting briefly and forcefully the program of Finnish liberalism. Inkilä, "Liberalismi," p. 109.
[34] *Ibid.*, pp. 108–109; Ståhlberg, *Puheita 1927–1946*, pp. 79–80.
[35] Ståhlberg, *Puheita 1927–1946*, p. 73.
[36] Ståhlberg, *Puheita 1883–1918*, pp. 12–13.
[37] Ståhlberg, *Puheita 1927–1946*, pp. 45–46.
[38] Mikkonen, "Ihminen," p. 309; Paavo Kastari, "K. J. Ståhlberg lainlaadintatyössä," in Tallgren, Salovius-Sinervo, and Laurila (editors), *Kaarlo Juho Ståhlberg*, p. 250.
[39] Ståhlberg, *Puheita 1883–1918*, p. 8.
[40] *Ibid.*, p. 12.

one's nationalism.[41] Although he believed that the Finnish language ought to gain the position appropriate to the language of almost nine-tenths of the population, Ståhlberg never favored revenge against the formerly dominant Swedish-speaking minority. During the years of Russification it became clear that *the* language question in Finland concerned Russian rather than Swedish.[42] In the constitution of 1919 Ståhlberg's moderation on the language question is apparent.[43] Swedish was given equal legal status with Finnish. During the interwar decades Ståhlberg stressed the need for constructive work on behalf of Finnish culture rather than the destructive desire for revenge that characterized some Finnish-speaking politicians.[44] His attitude earned him the hostility of the latter, but did not save him from being attacked as anti-Swedish by extremist Swedish-speaking Finns.[45]

Unlike many other Finnish nationalists, Ståhlberg considered the language question less important than constitutionalism. During Russification, for instance, he preferred to see constitutionalist Swedish-speaking Finns in high civil-service positions rather than have these positions filled by Finnish-speaking Finns not faithful to the Finnish constitution.[46] Nationalism he did not consider enough; liberalism, democracy, and constitutionalism were also necessary.[47] In 1905 Ståhlberg defined the political program which was his

[41] *Ibid.*, pp. 15, 225, 230; Ståhlberg, *Puheita 1927–1946*, p. 74.
[42] Ståhlberg, *Puheita 1883–1918*, p. 98.
[43] Puntila, *K. J. Ståhlberg*, p. 9.
[44] Ståhlberg, *Puheita 1927–1946*, p. 25. Ståhlberg's second wife (whom he married in 1920) had gone to a Swedish-language girls' school and never learned Finnish perfectly. Toini Havu, "Ester Ståhlberg," in Elsa Heporauta (editor), *Maan äitejä-kirja Suomen tasavallan presidenttien puolisoista* (Porvoo: Werner Söderström Osakeyhtiö, 1953), pp. 8–9.
[45] Jussi Teljo, *Suomen valtioelämän murros 1905–1908—Perustuslaillinen senaatti—viimeiset valtiopäivät—ensimmäinen eduskunta* (Porvoo: Werner Söderström Osakeyhtiö, 1949), p. 123.
[46] Ståhlberg, *Puheita 1883–1918*, p. 113.
[47] *Ibid.*, p. 25.

life's goal: *"democratic, liberal progress intended to raise the masses on the firm foundation of legality."* [48] Among his political values he gave his first place to constitutionalism. The rule of law was the precondition for political success [49] as well as for cultural and economic progress.[50]

Ståhlberg the politician was indistinguishable from Ståhlberg the jurist. The former Professor of Administrative Law was always evident, even in the most partisan situations. Ståhlberg's political speeches, in vocabulary and content, resemble the quiet words of a judge reaching a verdict in his chambers or of a teacher in his study rather than those of a demagogue in the forum. A former Prime Minister related that when he called upon President Ståhlberg he always had the feeling of a student going in to be examined by his teacher.[51] Ståhlberg generally appealed to reason rather than to instinct. Whenever he appealed to emotions, he invoked the integrating rather than the divisive feelings of human nature. It would, however, be a mistake to assume that Ståhlberg was a successful leader because he was a teacher by profession. "Leader" and "teacher" are not synonymous terms.[52] Scholarly judgment does not enable one to make decisions.[53] Although teaching is not leading, lead-

[48] *Ibid.*, p. 219.
[49] K. J. Ståhlberg, *Puheita 1919–1925* (Helsinki: Kustannusosakeyhtiö Otava, 1925), p. 105.
[50] Ståhlberg, *Puheita 1883–1918*, p. 149.
[51] Paavo Kastari, "K. J. Ståhlberg—Piirteitä lähikuvaan," *Suomalainen Suomi*, October, 1952, p. 389. A distinguished Finnish liberal referred to Ståhlberg as his master. Rudolf Holsti, "Maailmansodan aikaiset ulkopoliittiset suuntaukset Suomessa," in Tallgren, Salovius-Sinervo, and Laurila (editors), *Kaarlo Juho Ståhlberg*, p. 119. The most effective impressionistic description of Ståhlberg as the scholar in politics is given by Matti Kurjensaari, *Jäähyväiset 50-luvulle* (Helsinki: Kustannusosakeyhtiö Tammi, 1960), p. 173.
[52] Such an equation was suggested by Mary Parker Follett, "Leader and Expert," in Henry C. Metcalf and L. Urwick (editors), *Dynamic Administration: The Collected Papers of Mary Parker Follett* (New York; 1942), p. 267.
[53] Max Weber, "Science as a Vocation," in H. H. Gerth and C. Wright Mills (editors), *From Max Weber: Essays in Sociology* (New York, 1958),

ing may include an element of teaching: "To lead is to teach, and the leader occupies a pulpit from which he directs, for good or ill, the opinions and attitude of many thousands." [54] The theme of Ståhlberg's many lectures to the Finnish nation was the desirability of the rule of law. No audience was too large or too small for him to discuss that theme. The largest audience of Ståhlberg's long political career came in 1930, and the scholar in politics made effective use of the instructional opportunity presented by that situation. The former President of the Republic and his novelist wife were kidnapped by members of the extraparliamentary Lapua Movement. After they were driven seven hundred kilometers away from Helsinki toward the Soviet border, confusion among the kidnappers resulted in the release of the elderly victims. The short speech which Ståhlberg gave at the Helsinki railroad station upon their return from this frightening journey reflects, better than any academic analysis, his faith in the rule of law:

> Light and dark alternate in human life. . . . On one day, without legal security, deprived of constitutionally guaranteed freedom; on the next, breathing again the clean air of the legal social order, supported by the sure basis of the legal order. Whoever has experienced that has no doubt choosing, especially if he has, throughout his life, from decade to decade,

pp. 149–150; Stephen K. Bailey, *International Education: Shadow and Substance* (Cornell, 1963), p. 8; Adolf Hitler, *Mein Kampf* (translated by Ralph Manheim, Boston, 1943), p. 580; Henri Peyre, "Excellence and Leadership: Has Western Europe Any Lessons for Us?" *Daedalus*, Fall, 1961, pp. 630, 644–645; Erich Maria Remarque, *The Road Back* (translated by A. W. Wheen, New York, 1959), pp. 177–178; T. D. Weldon, *The Vocabulary of Politics* (Baltimore, 1960), pp. 149, 172; Kingsley Martin, *The Crown and the Establishment* (Harmondsworth, 1965), p. 180. The classic statement of this fact was made by a novelist: "Piggy could think. He could go step by step inside that fat head of his, only Piggy was no chief." William Golding, *Lord of the Flies* (New York, 1959), p. 97.

[54] William Bennett Munro, *Personality in Politics: Reformers, Bosses, and Leaders: What They Do and How They Do It* (New York, 1924), p. 113. See also John Morton Blum, *Woodrow Wilson and the Politics of Morality* (Boston, 1956), p. 199.

become ever more firmly convinced that a worthwhile human life for individual citizens, an orderly, peaceful, successful development for nations can best be obtained on the basis of a legal order in a democratic state. . . . The Finnish nation must hold fast to its legal order and its democratic constitution, and it will hold fast to them. In that faith we began our journey, and strengthened in that faith we again return to the capital of a free, independent Finland. Regardless and independent of the changes in our fates, a free, independent Finland will live, strong and fortunate. May it live long! [55]

In view of this strong belief in constitutionalism, it seems justifiable to assume that, in Ståhlberg's own judgment, his most important work was as chief author of the constitution of 1919. The work of the constitution makers in Central and Eastern Europe at the end of the First World War was largely in vain, but the Finnish constitution has survived to the present time. Controversial as it was at the time of its adoption, it is today questioned only by Communists.[56] Ståhlberg could therefore look back with satisfaction on his work in this respect. It was no exaggeration for him to conclude that the constitution was strong, durable, and appropriate for Finnish circumstances.[57]

Ståhlberg nevertheless recognized that a good constitution could not by itself guarantee good government. What mattered above all was the spirit which determined policy.[58] This spirit, at least in a democratic society, had to be the spirit of compromise. This was especially true in a multi-

[55] Ståhlberg, *Puheita 1927–1946*, pp. 13–14. For the first time, the former President wept in public on this occasion. Mikkonen, "Ihminen," p. 315.

[56] It is worth noting that in 1955 the chairmen of all parliamentary blocs introduced a bill to erect a statue of Ståhlberg in Helsinki. This bill was approved unanimously. *Helsingin Sanomat*, September 20, 1959. This unanimity contrasts with the political uproar created by the erection of a statue to Mannerheim.

[57] Ståhlberg, *Puheita 1883–1918*, p. 233; Ståhlberg, *Puheita 1919–1925*, p. 30; Ståhlberg, *Puheita 1927–1946*, pp. 36–38.

[58] Ståhlberg, *Puheita 1883–1918*, p. 176.

party system, where neither effective legislation nor cabinet stability was possible without widespread acceptance of the need for compromise.[59] As President of the Republic, Ståhlberg urged parliamentary leaders to be less rigid in their approach to other parties. In politics, after all, one must often sacrifice personal or partisan positions for the sake of achieving a common policy.[60] To emphasize this point, Ståhlberg said that as President he had to enforce the Prohibition Act, even though he earlier had opposed its adoption.[61] Even in relations with Russia compromise was desirable.[62]

The most controversial and revealing aspect of Ståhlberg's approach to compromise was his attitude toward the working class. He was distinctly middle-class in origin and affiliation: His father was a clergyman who died in his son's childhood, leaving his family in financial difficulties.[63] An admirer of K. J. Ståhlberg has referred to his victory in the presidential election of 1919 as the victory of the bourgeois middle class.[64] There is considerable justification for such an interpretation. Ståhlberg had been a member of the bourgeois estate, and he criticized the unicameral Parliament (which replaced the Four Estates in 1907) for containing too few businessmen.[65] He was an early President of the Finnish Bar Association. He never forgot that he had held important posts in all three branches of the Finnish civil service: administration, judiciary, and university.[66] He spoke out for the material interests of civil servants even as Presi-

[59] Ståhlberg, *Puheita 1919–1925*, p. 32.
[60] An amusing illustration of Ståhlberg's personal practice of compromise is given in *Presidenttikaskut—Kaskuja ja tarinoita tasavallan kahdeksasta päämiehestä* (Tampere: Kustannus Oy Lehmus, 1961), p. 18.
[61] Paavo Virkkunen, *Itsenäisen Suomen alkuvuosikymmeniltä—elettyä ja ajateltua* (Helsinki: Kustannusosakeyhtiä Otava, 1954), pp. 159–160.
[62] *Paasikiven muistelmia*, I, 64.
[63] Puntila, *K. J. Ståhlberg*, p. 3.
[64] Kurjensaari, *Taistelu*, p. 37.
[65] Ståhlberg, *Puheita 1883–1918*, p. 161.
[66] Ståhlberg, *Puheita 1919–1925*, p. 11.

dent.[67] It was appropriate that Ståhlberg was primarily a bureaucratic rather than a charismatic leader.[68] Nevertheless, as a leading Finnish conservative recognized, Ståhlberg was no White.[69] The latter rose above his own class origin and affiliation to become Finland's chief exponent of class peace, rather than class struggle. In Ståhlberg's political thought the dignity of man had a much higher value than capital.[70] Already during the period of Russification he was active in the labor affairs committees of Parliament and the City of Helsinki.[71] In sharp contrast to many other members of the Finnish bourgeoisie, Ståhlberg favored social reform without paternalism.[72] If necessary,

[67] *Ibid.*, pp. 25, 34, 37, 40.
[68] Kurjensaari, *Jäähyväiset*, p. 279.
[69] A. H. Saastamoinen, quoted by Virkkunen, *Itsenäisen*, p. 362. Characters in the greatest Finnish novel suggest that Ståhlberg was a secret Red. Väinö Linna, *Täällä Pohjantähden alla—toinen osa* (Porvoo: Werner Söderström Osakeyhtiö, 1960), p. 494; Linna, *Täällä Pohjantähden alla—kolmas osa* (Porvoo: Werner Söderström Osakeyhtiö, 1962), pp. 9, 294. This sentiment was no doubt shared by many of Ståhlberg's enemies who were members of the extreme right wing. The Finnish Communist Party, however, opposed Ståhlberg's election to the presidency in 1919 on the grounds that he would merely continue the policies of Regent Mannerheim. Hannu Soikkanen, *Työväenliikkeen jakautumisongelma itsenäisyyden alkuvuosina*, reprinted from *Turun Historiallisen Yhdistyksen julkaisuja*, XV, 279. A leading Communist intellectual later awarded Ståhlberg the title of "people's" President on the basis of his support in 1919 as well as his policies while in office. Raoul Palmgren, "Kansan ja herrojen presidentit, vahvat ja heikot presidentit," *Tilanne*, December, 1961, p. 57.
[70] Laurila, "K. J. Ståhlberg," p. 303.
[71] Axel Bergholm (editor), *Keisarillisen Suomen Hallituskonseljin ja Senaatin puheenjohtajat, jäsenet ja virkamiehet 1809-1909—biograafisia tietoja* (Porvoo: Werner Söderstrom Osakeyhtiö, 1912), p. 397; Yrjö Harvia, "K. J. Ståhlberg kunnallismiehenä," in Tallgren, Salovius-Sinervo, and Laurila (editors), *Kaarlo Juho Ståhlberg*, pp. 67–68. Detailed statements of Ståhlberg's favorable attitude toward social reform already during the period of Russification are his *Tyttömyysvakuutuksesta* (Helsinki: Kustannusosakeyhtiö Otava, 1903); *Työriitain sovittaminen ja ratkaiseminen—lausunto Helsingin kaupungin työväenasiain lautakunnalle* (Helsinki: Kustannusosakeyhtiö Otava, 1905); *Työriitain sovittaminen ja ratkaiseminen* (Porvoo: Werner Söderström Osakeyhtiö, 1912).
[72] Ståhlberg, *Puheita 1883-1918*, pp. 63–64.

social reforms should be enacted in a speedy and sweeping fashion.[73] As Minister of Commerce and Industry in 1905–1907, he supported the principle of collective-bargaining agreements.[74] Ståhlberg did not permit the Finnish Civil War of 1918 to dampen his enthusiasm for social reform. He warned against a conservative reaction to the Civil War which would impede social progress. The working class should not pay for its mistakes in 1918 by losing all chance to better its condition.[75] Both during and after his presidency Ståhlberg supported a policy of reconciliation that attempted to reintegrate the working class, defeated in 1918, into the Finnish nation.[76] The success of this policy was substantial.[77] The impact upon future Finnish politics of the relatively stable social milieu of the nineteen-twenties can hardly be overemphasized.[78] The crucial test came in the Winter War, when the working class was one with the Finnish nation in fighting the Soviet Union.

As a result of his belief in compromise, Ståhlberg accepted both the inevitability and the desirability of political parties. Without parties progress would be unthinkable.[79]

[73] *Ibid.*, p. 96.

[74] Kurjensaari, *Taistelu*, pp. 35–36; Matti Kurjensaari, "K. J. Ståhlberg—tasavallan perustaja," in Matti Kuusi (editor), *Suomen tasavallan presidentit* (Porvoo: Werner Söderström Osakeyhtiö, 1960), p. 23; Leo Ehrnrooth, "K. J. Ståhlberg senaatin kauppa- ja teollisuustoimituskunnan päällikkönä," in Tallgren, Salovius-Sinervo, and Laurila (editors), *Kaarlo Juho Ståhlberg*, pp. 75–93.

[75] Ståhlberg, *Puheita 1883–1918*, p. 193; Ståhlberg, *Puheita 1919–1925*, pp. 162–163, 167–168, 174.

[76] Ståhlberg, *Puheita 1927–1946*, pp. 24–25, 36.

[77] Vilkuna (editor), *Maan*, pp. 259–260; Einar Böök, "Sosiaalipoliittista toimintaa Suomessa itsenäisyyden alkuvuosina," in Tallgren, Salovius-Sinervo, and Laurila (editors), *Kaarlo Juho Ståhlberg*, pp. 220–228.

[78] That Ståhlberg's policy of reconciliation was not completely successful is apparent from the strength of Finnish Communism, which during the interwar decades derived largely from the heritage of 1918. This strength is analyzed in my article, "The Problem of Generations in Finnish Communism," *The American Slavic and East European Review*, XVII (April, 1958), 190–202.

[79] Ståhlberg, *Puheita 1883–1918*, pp. 40, 83, 119.

Already in 1908 Ståhlberg wrote that the abolition of parties was both impossible and undesirable. Neither the present situation nor future progress was conceivable without parties.[80] The only alternative to the competition of political parties in the twentieth century is totalitarianism, in which only one party is permitted.[81] Unlike the Finnish extreme right wing, which demanded that the Social Democratic Party be declared illegal, Ståhlberg argued that Social Democracy was not only a constructive political force, but was compatible with patriotism.[82]

Only through parliamentary government, in Ståhlberg's judgment, could distortion of the popular will be avoided.[83] He therefore firmly advocated adoption in Finland of the principle of parliamentary government.[84] He repeatedly defended the competence and efficiency of the Finnish Parliament.[85] Ståhlberg's support of parliamentary government was not confined to words. In 1907, at a time when the principle of parliamentary government was unknown in Finnish political practice, he informed members of the new unicameral Parliament that the Mechelin Cabinet, of which he was a leading member, would resign if it did not possess the confidence of Parliament.[86] A few months later, Parliament adopted a far more sweeping Prohibition Act than that submitted by Ståhlberg, then Minister of Commerce and Industry. Ståhlberg resigned. According to his own statement, this resignation was intended to advance the case of parlia-

---

[80] Laurila, "K. J. Ståhlberg," p. 295. Indicative of Ståhlberg's institutional approach to politics is the fact that he quite mistakenly thought that the Finnish multiparty system was caused by proportional representation. Ståhlberg, *Parlamentarismi*, p. 69.
[81] Ståhlberg, *Puheita 1927–1946*, pp. 93–94.
[82] *Ibid.*, pp. 29, 92–93.
[83] *Ibid.*, p. 94.
[84] Ståhlberg, *Puheita 1883–1918*, pp. 150, 167.
[85] *Ibid.*, pp. 145–146; Ståhlberg, *Puheita 1919–1925*, p. 104; Ståhlberg, *Puheita 1927–1946*, p. 36; Ståhlberg, *Parlamentarismi*, p. 88.
[86] Ståhlberg, *Puheita 1883–1918*, p. 69.

mentary government.[87] Urho Kekkonen, later President of the Republic, argued that Ståhlberg in 1907 first put into practice in Finland the principle of parliamentary government.[88] This principle was not further implemented during the remaining decade of Russification. It was not until 1917 that parliamentary government triumphed in Finland. Since then, written explicitly into the 1919 constitution, parliamentary government has been the basic institutional fact of Finnish politics.

A belief in compromise, of course, sometimes serves as an excuse for weak and indecisive leadership in democratic political systems. Ståhlberg did not fall prey to this temptation. The vigor of his leadership as first occupant of the powerful office of President of the Republic was undeniable. Ståhlberg used his legal powers to the utmost. At a meeting of the Council of State the Minister of Justice refused to convey to Parliament a bill granting amnesty to those defeated in the Civil War of 1918. This bill was supported by the majority of the Cabinet as well as by the President. Ståhlberg immediately announced that the recalcitrant minister was removed from office, and that the Minister of Interior, an enthusiastic supporter of amnesty, was Acting Minister of Justice.[89] After the arrest of the Communist parliamentary bloc in 1923, the question of holding a new election arose. In opposition to Ståhlberg, Prime Minister

[87] *Ibid.*, p. 116. It has been later argued that Ståhlberg's motivation in resigning was not connected with the principle of parliamentary government. L. A. Puntila, "Parlamentaarisen järjestelmän alkuvaiheet ja parlamentarismi itsenäisyyden aikana," in Pentti Renvall (editor), *Suomalaisen kansanvallan kehitys* (Porvoo: Werner Söderström Osakeyhtiö, 1956), p. 181. Not only did Ståhlberg state that he intended by his action to demonstrate his faithfulness to the principle of parliamentary government, but his political rivals accepted this interpretation. Teljo, *Suomen*, p. 220; *Paasikiven muistelmia*, II, 33. In a later work, Puntila appears to retract his previous interpretation. L. A. Puntila, *Suomen poliittinen historia 1809–1955* (Helsinki: Kustannusosakeyhtiö Otava, 1964), p. 90.
[88] Vilkuna (editor), *Maan*, p. 260.
[89] Virkkunen, *Itsenäisen*, p. 100.

Kyösti Kallio favored delaying this election.[90] The President forced the resignation of the Cabinet, and appointed a caretaker Cabinet, which supported the immediate dissolution of Parliament.[91] Such exercises of presidential power were by no means extraordinary during Ståhlberg's tenure in office.[92] They flowed from his conception of the Cabinet as the President's "responsible advisers."[93] Ståhlberg, undoubtedly, was one of the most energetic and effective Finnish Presidents.[94]

Ståhlberg's strong leadership as President did not lead to unpopularity. He could undoubtedly have been reelected, perhaps unanimously, in 1925, had he chosen to run. Even those who had supported the monarchy in 1918, and Mannerheim in 1919, later conceded that the right man had been elected President in that year.[95] They admired Ståhlberg as "a man who knew what he wanted and explained his will in a way that it was difficult to oppose on factual grounds" and who also "carried out his will with the support of the constitution."[96] In 1925 Ståhlberg was assured of support by his former opponents in the National Coalition Party if he chose to accept reelection. His attitude toward another term, however, was that he would not, in contrast to the retired diva, give another performance.[97]

[90] Juho Niukkanen in Parliament, *1930 Valtiopäivät, Pöytäkirjat*, p. 1020.
[91] Ståhlberg, *Parlamentarismi*, pp. 65–67; Virkkunen, *Itsenäisen*, pp. 61–62, 99–100; Puntila, "Parlamentaarisen," pp. 183–184.
[92] Kurjensaari, "K. J. Ståhlberg," p. 28.
[93] Ståhlberg, *Puheita 1919–1925*, p. 109.
[94] Paavo Kastari, *Tasavallan presidentin asema* (Porvoo: Werner Söderström Osakeyhtiö, 1961), pp. 26, 59–62; Raoul Palmgren, "Kansan ja herrojen presidentit, vahvat ja heikot presidentit," *Tilanne*, December, 1961, p. 59; Puntila, *Suomen poliittinen historia*, p. 199.
[95] Virkkunen, *Itsenäisen*, p. 69.
[96] *Ibid.*, p. 100.
[97] *Ibid.*, p. 64; Hirvikallio, *Tasavallan*, pp. 20–21, 25, 34–35; Puntila, *Suomen poliittinen historia*, p. 153. It is entirely misleading to suggest that Ståhlberg did not seek reelection because collaboration ended between center and left parties, as do Eino Jutikkala and Kauko Pirinen, *A History of Finland* (translated by Paul Sjöblom, New York, 1962), p. 270.

The rise of the antiparliamentary Lapua Movement in the winter of 1929/30 [98] brought Ståhlberg back on the Finnish political scene. He attacked the Lapua Movement in numerous speeches and articles.[99] In order to demonstrate his support of parliamentary government, he became a candidate for Parliament.[100] The Lapua Movement considered Ståhlberg the embodiment of its opposition,[101] as did that opposition.[102] Vihtori Kosola, the leader of the Lapua Movement, publicly threatened a settling of accounts with Ståhlberg.[103] This threat was carried out shortly after Ståhlberg was elected to Parliament, when the former President and his wife were kidnapped by agents of the Lapua Movement.[104] The movement's attitude toward the kidnapping was stated with considerable precision.

Everyone certainly agreed that Professor Ståhlberg was rightly and deservedly kidnapped, since it was precisely he who was one of those most guilty for the decline of our country's domestic and foreign policy position into the existing misuse of

[98] The political thought, action, and organization of this movement are analyzed in my study of *Three Generations: The Extreme Right Wing in Finnish Politics* (Bloomington, 1962).

[99] The most important of these were a series of signed articles in Finland's largest newspaper, the *Helsingin Sanomat*—especially June 26, 1930—and a Helsinki election campaign speech of September 7, 1930, reprinted in Ståhlberg, *Puheita 1927–1946*, pp. 87–102. Ståhlberg's statements attacking the Lapua Movement were published in pamphlet form as *Kaksi kirjoitusta ja kaksi puhetta* (Helsinki: Helsingin Uusi Kirjapaino Oy, 1930).

[100] Ståhlberg, *Puheita 1927–1946*, pp. 35–36.

[101] Hirvikallio, *Tasavallan*, p. 46; "P. E. Svinhufvud presidentiksi," *Itsenäinen Suomi*, 1931 (Number 1), p. 2; "Ei mitään tinkimistä," *Itsenäinen Suomi*, 1931 (Number 2), p. 16; Linna, *Täällä Pohjantähden alla*, p. 260.

[102] R. Palomeri [Raoul Palmgren], *30-luvun kuvat* (Helsinki: Kustannusosakeyhtiö Tammi, n. d.), pp. 84, 114.

[103] *Iltalehti*, September 19, 1930.

[104] A foreign observer later drew the remarkable conclusion that the Ståhlbergs "were to be taken across the Soviet border and there murdered, charging the crime to a Bolshevik assassination and a just cause for Finno-Soviet armed conflict." Gregory Meiksins, *The Baltic Riddle: Finland, Estonia, Latvia, Lithuania—Key-points of European Peace* (New York, 1943), p. 148.

democracy. In addition, there were many bitter memories of him from the years before the War of Independence and from his presidency, even though they could not be expressed so long as he remained *the country's former President.* Now, when he again came on the scene as the very same standard bearer of that liberalism, leading to disaster, of which there were already bitter enough experiences, he too could be judged according to his deeds. He could no longer be the former President and, in that capacity, inviolable.[105]

The response of the vast majority of Finns to this kidnapping however, was different. It was considered one of the most shameful events in Finnish history, even by the press and political leaders opposed to Ståhlberg's policies.[106] The public reaction to this crime was the most important single factor in reducing the chances of the Lapua Movement's coming into power.[107] This fact was recognized by the leader of the Social Democratic Party:

> This trip by the former President of the Republic was, of course, a melancholy trip, and we are all surely ready to protest from our hearts against it, but, on the other hand, we should be very grateful for it to him, for a more effective political agitation trip has never taken place in this country.[108]

In the presidential election of 1931, which took place several months after the kidnapping, Ståhlberg's electoral slate

[105] Artturi Vuorimaa, *Kolme kuukautta Kosolassa—Lapuan liikkeen pesässä nähtyä, kuultua ja kuviteltua* (Lapua: Artturi Vuorimaa, 1931), pp. 117–118. The leader of the Lapua Movement demonstrated that the movement was fundamentally anti-liberal rather than anti-Communist (as it claimed) when he stated that "Ståhlberg's policy gave birth to the Lapua Movement." Vihtori Kosola, interviewed by *Ajan Sana,* February 4, 1931.

[106] Prime Minister P. E. Svinhufvud to Parliament, *1930 Toiset Valtiopäivät, Pöytäkirjat,* pp. 11, 26, 29; President Lauri Relander to Parliament, *ibid.,* p. 19; Uuno Hannula, *"Me teemmee, mitä tahdomme"* (Helsinki: Helsingin Uusi Kirjapaino-Osakeyhtiö, 1933), pp. 21–22.

[107] Mikkonen, "Ihminen," pp. 315–316; Vilkuna (editor), *Maan,* p. 262; Linna, *Täällä Pohjantähden alla,* III, 293, 314.

[108] Väinö Tanner in Parliament, *1930 Toiset Valtiopäivät, Pöytäkirjat,* p. 44.

drew a surprisingly large vote, 17.7 percent of the total votes cast, compared with only 5.8 percent for National Progressive Party candidates in the 1930 parliamentary election.[109] This increase can be regarded as a popular vote of confidence in Ståhlberg after his kidnapping. Ståhlberg, according to his own statement, never regretted his party affiliation.[110] Although he approved of the existence of a party system, and remained loyal to his own party, partisanship was for him only a means to an end. He hoped that the National Progressive Party—in a fundamental sense, *his* party—would continue to exist and even to grow in terms of popular support. If this party had to choose between losing popular support or compromising its principles, however, Ståhlberg was prepared to risk a reduction in party membership.[111] Compromise should never become *Kompromiss*. The ultimate responsibility of a political leader was not to his party or his class or even his nation, but to himself. The personal honor which a leader possessed was the only real guarantee of the correctness of his action. If he did not place honor above power, he did not belong in politics. K. J. Ståhlberg fulfilled his own high standards in this respect. He preferred to lose his high post in the civil service in 1903 rather than participate in illegal Russification policies. As a Director of the Bank of Finland, he refused to turn over the Bank's assets to Red Guards during the Civil War of 1918.[112] The Lapua Movement, after the kidnapping, publicly threatened his assassination,[113] but this did not reduce Ståhlberg's determination to defend parliamentary govern-

[109] *Suomen virallinen tilasto—XXIX. Vaalitilasto. A 16. Tasavallan presidentin valitsijamiesten vaalit vuonna 1931*, pp. 16–17. On the third and final ballot the electoral college gave Ståhlberg 149 (out of a total of 300) votes and P. E. Svinhufvud 151. In 1937, Ståhlberg again failed in the electoral college, although he received 150 (of 300) votes on the first ballot.

[110] Ståhlberg, *Puheita 1883–1918*, p. 226.

[111] Ståhlberg, *Puheita 1927–1946*, pp. 9–10, 12.

[112] Juhani Paasivirta, *Suomi vuonna 1918* (Porvoo: Werner Söderström Osakeyhtiö, 1957), p. 72; Mikkonen, "Ihminen," p. 311.

[113] "Laukauksia," *Aktivisti*, February 14, 1931.

ment. In 1945 he advised the Finnish Government that the "war responsibility" trials demanded by the Soviet Union were unconstitutional.[114]

An American author has argued that Ståhlberg was "somewhat embarrassed" by his victory over Gustaf Mannerheim in the presidential election of 1919.[115] If so, Ståhlberg's inaugural address was deceptive in its confidence.[116] He may have preferred principle to power, but when these two were compatible, and especially when, as in 1930, principle demanded competing for office, he openly sought power. It is unlikely that either K. J. Ståhlberg or the Finnish nation was ever embarrassed by his possession of political power. It may well be that nineteenth-century liberalism is no longer meaningful in twentieth-century politics, in Finland as elsewhere. In a world of permanent revolution, nevertheless, Finland maintained both parliamentary government and national independence. This fact is not due to any miracle, but a possible partial explanation lies in one man's faith. When K. J. Ståhlberg completed his secondary-school education, his rector wrote in the student register: *Spes nostratium et decus*. This judgment of the student is equally applicable to the scholar in politics.

[114] K. J. Ståhlberg, *Lausuntoja* (Helsinki: Kustannusosakeyhtiö Otava, 1947), pp. 24–26; Hyvämäki, *Vaaran*, pp. 48, 50, 63; Yrjö Soini, *Kuin Pietari hiilivalkealla—Sotasyyllisyysasian vaiheet 1944–1949* (Helsinki: Kustannusosakeyhtiö Otava, 1956), pp. 49–52.

[115] C. Jay Smith, Jr., *Finland and the Russian Revolution 1917–1922* (Athens, 1958), p. 158. Another writer did not even bother to give the name of the victor when discussing the presidential election of 1919, alluding merely to "a civilian." H. B. Elliston, *Finland Fights* (Boston, 1940), p. 86. Ståhlberg fared only slightly better at the hands of another writer who referred to Mannerheim's successful opponent in 1919 as "a professor who had also played a brave part in the War of Independence." Rosita Forbes, *These Men I Knew* (New York, 1940), p. 280.

[116] Ståhlberg, *Puheita 1919–1925*, pp. 7–8; *1919 Valtiopäivät, Pöytäkirjat*, I, 1086.

# V

## ✯ ✯ ✯ ✯
## The Politician in Politics: J. K. Paasikivi

The approaching end of the Russo-Finnish War in 1944 created a crisis in the leadership of the Finnish political system. The awful truth became apparent: Finnish foreign policy based upon open antagonism to the Soviet Union could only lead to the end of national independence and parliamentary government. The situation was critical, in that the patient was near death. If the Finnish political system were to survive, new leaders were needed to replace those who had exercised power during the war and who had brought Finland to the brink of destruction. Most of these wartime leaders insisted on the correctness of their previous policy. It was only the military collapse of the Finnish Army in the summer of 1944 which finally forced them to make peace with the Soviet Union. Soviet leaders, in turn, were unwilling to depend upon the wartime Finnish leaders for execution of the severe armistice terms. It was therefore necessary to find new leadership which would be willing to assume responsibility in a perilous situation, which would have the confidence of both Finns and Russians, and which could effectively work toward peaceful relations between Finland and the Soviet Union. These prerequisites meant the automatic exclusion of Finnish Communists, in whom most Finns did not have confidence, and of most of those who had played prominent roles in Finnish politics after 1939, in whom Soviet leaders did not have confidence.

This crisis in leadership was successfully resolved by the selection of Gustaf Mannerheim as President of the Republic and J. K. Paasikivi as Prime Minister. This resolution was, at first glance, remarkable. Instead of leading to a movement to the left, the Finnish military defeat brought to the top of the political system two elderly conservatives, one a former general in the Russian Imperial Army and the other a former leading banker, who had both been monarchists in 1918 and whose opposition to Marxism was overwhelming. These two men ended their long careers by successfully defending national independence and parliamentary government, even though neither had worked for independence before 1917 and both were contemptuous of parliamentary government long after it was first implemented in that year. Neither K. J. Ståhlberg nor Väinö Tanner, both of whom were dedicated above all to national independence and parliamentary government, was able to adjust adequately to the lesson of 1944. It remained for their old opponents to achieve their goals. The unyielding legalism of Ståhlberg and the equally unyielding anti-Russian feelings of Tanner were not enough to meet the need for realism. The ultimate irony was provided by the Soviet Government, which permitted Finland to choose a President who considered his life's mission to be the struggle against Bolshevism, while in the Kremlin Otto Kuusinen, who had faithfully served international Communism for three decades, waited in vain for the triumphant return to Finland that would never occur.

Mannerheim's increasing physical incapacity, after five exhausting years as a septuagenarian Commander-in-Chief, meant that most day-to-day decisions of his presidency were left to Paasikivi, whose dominant position was finally "legitimized" when he succeeded Mannerheim as President in 1946. Throughout his presidency, until his retirement in 1956, Paasikivi was the central figure in Finnish politics. The period 1944–1956 was recognized as the Paasikivi era by his opponents [1] as well as his supporters.[2] Among those recognizing the unity which Paasikivi's leadership gave to Finnish politics was the President himself. Upon retiring from the presidency in 1956 Paasikivi told the Finnish Parliament: "One period in the life of our nation, which began with the close of the wars,[3] now ends."[4]

That an entire historical period of a decisive nature in Finnish politics should be named after Paasikivi was perhaps appropriate, for his dominant intellectual interest was the study of history.[5] Particularly, the lives of significant political leaders in widely separated times and places were the object of Paasikivi's detailed scrutiny.[6] No other major Finnish political leader has had so profound an interest in, and knowledge of, the European past.[7] The political leader

[1] Edwin Linkomies, "J. K. Paasikivi" *Valvoja*, 1957, p. 2; Pauli Burman and Matti Nieminen, *Osakeyhtiö Isänmaa* (Jyväskylä: K. J. Gummerus Osakeyhtiö, 1959), pp. 44, 49.

[2] Matti Kurjensaari, "'Paasikiven aikakausi,'" in Kauko Kare (editor), *J. K. Paasikivi. Itsenäisyys—rauha—valtiollinen sivistys* (Hämeenlinna: Arvi A. Karisto Osakeyhtiö, 1960), p. 139; see also L. A. Puntila, *Suomen poliittinen historia 1809–1955* (Helsinki: Kustannusosakeyhtiö Otava, 1964), p. 216.

[3] By using the plural rather than the singular Paasikivi indicated that he considered that Finland had engaged in two separate wars, the first in 1939–1940 and the second in 1941–1944. Apologists for wartime Finnish policy argue that the second war was merely a logical continuation of the first, waged to rectify the injustice of the peace settlement of 1940.

[4] *Paasikiven linja I—Juho Kusti Paasikiven puheita vuosilta 1944–1956* (Porvoo: Werner Söderström Osakeyhtiö, 1956), p. 213.

[5] V. J. Sukselainen, "A Statesman's Life," *Finlandia Review* (Helsinki: The Finnish Foreign Trade Association [1957]), p. 34; Puntila, *Suomen poliittinen historia*, p. 189.

[6] Paasikivi would undoubtedly have nodded his assent to the argument that "the Founding Fathers thought history too serious a business to be left to the historians. It was the concern of all, but especially of statesmen—just the view that Winston Churchill took all of his life." Henry Steele Commager, "Leadership in Eighteenth-Century America and Today," *Daedalus*, fall 1961, p. 661.

[7] That there were significant gaps in Paasikivi's understanding of non-European areas, even the United States, is apparent in *Paasikiven linja II—Juho Kusti Paasikiven puheita ja esitelmiä vousilta 1923–1942* (Porvoo:

publicly proclaimed himself to be a historian,[8] and during his last years his favorite reception place for foreign journalists was his study, filled with a vast range of historical monographs and biographies, mostly in the original languages. In the final months before his death Clemenceau's memoirs were his favorite.[9] This was not merely public posturing, for scholarly investigation of Paasikivi's personal library after his death revealed a very large number of closely read, and frequently annotated, historical studies. Particularly well-represented were books on Russian history, ranging in subject from Maximilian Braun's *Der Aufstieg Russlands vom Wikingerstaat zur europäischen Grossmacht* to Isaac Deutscher's *Russia after Stalin*.[10]

In spite of the fact that Paasikivi eventually completed his graduate studies in law rather than history, the Finnish scholars who most significantly influenced his political thought, beginning—but not ending—in his student days, were two conservative historians, G. Z. Yrjö-Koskinen and J. R. Danielson-Kalmari. Paasikivi considered the latter to be the person closest to himself intellectually.[11] In 1891, as a

Werner Söderström Osakeyhtiö, 1956), pp. 197, 205; J. K. Paasikivi, *Valtio ja talouselämä* (Helsinki: Suomalaisen Kirjallisuuden Seuran Kirjapainon Oy, 1935), p. 15.

[8] *Paasikiven linja*, I, 56.

[9] Ida Pekari, "Lukulamppu, kävelykeppi, frakki—Hellstenin pojasta tasavallan päämieheksi," in Kare (editor), *J. K. Paasikivi*, p. 138.

[10] Kerttu Tanner, "J. K. Paasikivi kirjastonsa valossa," *Historiallinen aikakauskirja*, 1960 (Number 4), pp. 477–478.

[11] L. A. Puntila, *J. K. Paasikiven linja* (Helsinki: Hämäläis-Osakunta, 1957), p. 6. From 1903 to 1910 Paasikivi and Danielson-Kalmari were in daily contact, living in the same apartment house. *Paasikiven muistelmia sortovuosilta*, I (Porvoo: Werner Söderström Osakeyhtiö, 1957), p. 2. Two decades after his friend's death Paasikivi described him as "unforgettable." *Paasikiven linja*, I, 143. Given the fact that the relationship between Danielson-Kalmari and Paasikivi was that of teacher to student, it was unlikely that the former could qualify as the latter's best friend. This position undoubtedly was occupied by Ernst Nevanlinna, a conservative economist and politician, who became a university student in the same year (1890) as Paasikivi, and who remained on intimate terms with the latter until Nevanlinna's death in 1932. *Paasikiven linja*, II, 78; *Paasikiven muistelmia*

young university student, Paasikivi studied in Novgorod, hoping to become, like Danielson-Kalmari before him, a professional historian, specializing in Russian relations with Finland and Sweden.[12] From this study of Russian history, Paasikivi, with Gustaf Mannerheim and other members of the generation of older conservatives, learned the possibility of good relations between Russia and Finland.

Paasikivi's historical orientation was primarily responsible for determining his reaction to the threat of Russification of Finland which was presented by the Grand Duke's policies after 1899. Finnish jurists and historians responded to this challenge in fundamentally different ways. Jurists, in the Young Finnish Party, stressed the legal rights of Finnish autonomy guaranteed by the Russian Emperor when he became Grand Duke of Finland in 1809. Historians, in the Old Finnish Party, emphasized the overwhelming difference between Russian and Finnish power. In this controversy Paasikivi, despite his legal training, emphatically sided with the historians. In his view, historians saw this particular policy problem differently from jurists, just as these two groups see the world generally from different perspectives.[13] Paasikivi was fond of referring to Ranke's argument that historians see events *wie es gewesen ist,* not as moral questions.[14] Legal provisions ought not to dominate in policy making.[15] The

*sortovuosilta,* II (Porvoo: Werner Söderström Osakeyhtiö, 1957), p. 214; Pekari, "Lukulamppu," pp. 130–131.

[12] *Paasikiven linja,* I, 183.

[13] Paasikivi's position was essentially similar to that of Hugh Trevor-Roper, who referred to the distinction between realistic and utopian political attitudes, and added: "If these are the terms we are to use, I must declare myself a realist, not a utopian; but then I am a historian, and I suppose all historians are realists in politics; at least I cannot imagine what the works of a utopian historian would be like." "Human Nature in Politics—II," *The Listener,* December 10, 1953, p. 993.

[14] *Paasikiven muistelmia,* I, 39.

[15] *Paasikiven linja,* II, 109, 118; *Paasikiven muistelmia,* I, 27; *Paasikiven muistelmia,* II, 75, 160, 196; J. K. Paasikivi, *Talo on korjattava, ei revittävä* (Helsinki: Suomalaisen Kirjallisuuden Seuran Kirjapainon Oy., 1936), p. 22; J. K. Paasikivi, *Toimintani Moskovassa ja Suomessa 1939–41.*

essence of Paasikivi's political thought was that legal advocacy should not be confused with political considerations.[16] Appropriately, Paasikivi's personal copy of a French translation of Machiavelli's *Prince* was carefully studied.[17] One of the dominant themes running throughout Paasikivi's conversations, speeches, and writings was the need for realism in politics, especially in the foreign policy of a small nation.[18] In his view, the first rule of politics is to accept as facts those things which cannot be changed—to recognize necessity.[19] One of those facts is that, given the existing state of international politics, it is useless to speak of moral principles and human values when one has to deal with questions of foreign policy.[20] In his Independence Day speech in December, 1944, Prime Minister Paasikivi recalled Macaulay's argument that understanding of realities is the beginning of wisdom.[21] Political actions are to be judged by their consequences, not by their intentions.[22] Paasikivi's realism was in distinct contrast to a long tradition of emo-

---

1—*Talvisota* (Porvoo: Werner Söderström Osakeyhtiö, 1958), pp. 58, 60–61, 216; J. K. Paasikivi, *Toimintani Moskovassa ja Suomessa 1939–41. II—välirauhan aika* (Porvoo: Werner Söderström Osakeyhtiö, 1958), pp. 37–38, 41, 91, 101, 104.

[16] Matti Kekkonen and Jouko Tyyri, *Asiat ja asenteet* (Jyväskylä: K. J. Gummerus Osakeyhtiö, 1959), p. 90.

[17] Tanner, "J. K. Paasikivi," p. 475; see also *ibid.*, p. 481; Paasikivi, *Toimintani*, I, 58; Paasikivi, *Toimintani*, II, 86.

[18] Matti Mannerkorpi, "Tarton rauhasta Porkkalan palauttamiseen—J. K. Paasikivi itsenäisyyden ja rauhan turvaajana 1921–1956," in Kare (editor), *J. K. Paasikivi*, pp. 70, 79; Iisakki Laati, "Rauhanneuvottelija Paasikivi," in *ibid.*, p. 99; Kurjensaari, "'Paasikiven aikakausi,'" p. 144; Urho Kekkonen, "J. K. Paasikivi—rauhantekijä-presidentti," in Matti Kuusi (editor), *Suomen tasavallan presidentit* (Porvoo: Werner Söderström Osakeyhtiö 1960), pp. 195–196; *Paasikiven linja*, I, 14, 99, 203; *Paasikiven linja*, II, 78; *Paasikiven muistelmia*, I, 50, 224–225, *Paasikiven muistelmia*, II, 159–160; Paasikivi, *Toimintani*, I, 8–9, 16, 92, 94; Paasikivi, *Toimintani*, II, 4, 10, 13, 91, 100, 165–166, 175, 182, 186.

[19] Paasikivi, *Toimintani*, II, 192.

[20] Paasikivi, *Toimintani*, I, 35.

[21] *Paasikiven linja*, I, 9; see also Paasikivi, *Toimintani*, I, 199.

[22] *Paasikiven muistelmia*, I, 35.

tionalism in the Finnish approach to foreign policy.[23] This tradition was perhaps best exemplified in the instructions given by Foreign Minister Eljas Erkko to Paasikivi as the latter departed for Moscow in the fateful autumn of 1939: "Forget that Russia is a great power." [24]

Understandably, the dichotomy between official Finnish policy and Paasikivi's realism led to harsh criticism by him of that policy. In his view, throughout the interwar decades Finnish policy toward the Soviet Union was essentially mistaken.[25] The Treaty of Dorpat (1920) drew the border too close to Leningrad, thus creating legitimate Soviet fears for the security of that city.[26] The secret Soviet demands of 1938 were arbitrarily dismissed by the Finnish Government.[27] The Winter War could have been avoided had it not been for the errors of Finnish policy.[28] This policy was based on "illusions" [29] because the Finnish ship of state "lacked leadership." [30] "Naïve" public opinion was permitted to determine policy.[31] During the Winter War this state of affairs continued.[32] The lack of leadership led di-

[23] *Paasikiven linja*, I, 30, 91; Matti Kurjensaari, *Jäähyväiset 50-luvulle* (Helsinki: Kustannusosakeyhtiö Tammi, 1960), pp. 17, 156; *Paasikiven muistelmia*, I, 5, 131; *Paasikiven muistelmia*, II, 192–193; Paasikivi, *Toimintani*, I, 16, 55, 58, 75, 125, 131; Paasikivi, *Toimintani*, II, 58, 182, 184; Puntila, *Suomen poliittinen historia*, p. 135.
[24] Paasikivi, *Tomintani*, I, 58.
[25] *Paasikiven muistelmia*, I, 76–77; Tanner, "J. K. Paasikivi," p. 478.
[26] *Paasikiven muistelmia*, I, 76; *Paasikiven linja* I, 46–47, 57, 196; Toivo Heikkilä, *Paasikivi peräsimessä—pääministerin sihteerin muistelmat 1944–1948* (Helsinki: Kustannusosakeyhtiö Otava, 1965), p. 94.
[27] *Paasikiven muistelmia*, I, 77; Paasikivi, *Toimintani*, I, 8. Paasikivi was not informed of these demands at the time they were first made. Mannerkorpi, "Tarton rauhasta," p. 65.
[28] *Paasikiven muistelmia*, I, 64, 77; *Paasikiven linja*, I, 36, 47, 57; Paasikivi, *Toimintani*, I, 9, 16, 86–87, 94, 97, 109, 117; Paasikivi, *Toimintani*, II, 5, 29, 182–184; Reinhold Svento, *Ystäväni Juho Kusti Paasikivi* (Porvoo: Werner Söderström Osakeyhtiö, 1960), pp. 68–69.
[29] Paasikivi, *Toimintani*, II, 58.
[30] *Ibid.*, p. 116.
[31] Paasikivi, *Toimintani*, I, 99; see also *ibid.*, pp. 114, 147.
[32] *Ibid.*, pp. 135, 146–147, 155.

rectly to the Treaty of Moscow (1940), whose provisions were the heaviest blow that the Finnish nation had ever suffered.[33] Even after the Finnish military collapse of 1940, the Finnish Government continued to live in a "dream world."[34] Paasikivi, therefore in February, 1941, sent a sharply worded private message to the Foreign Minister, resigning as Finnish Minister in Moscow because he did not wish to have "even the most remote connection with a policy which may lead to catastrophe."[35] As a private citizen, Paasikivi opposed Finnish policy in the Russo-Finnish War of 1941–1944, and was especially critical of the Finnish invasion of East Karelia, which had never been part of Finland.[36] Almost alone among major Finnish political leaders, he foresaw Finland's fate if National Socialist Germany won the Second World War.[37] To remove his embarrassing presence from his homeland, the Finnish Government attempted unsuccessfully to send him on an aimless mission to Switzerland.[38] Until the autumn of 1944 Paasikivi was without office and without power; for all practical purposes, he had no followers. When, in the summer of 1944, the Finnish Government finally decided to seek a separate peace with the Soviet Union, he thought an armistice agreement could

[33] *Ibid.*, p. 205.

[34] Paasikivi, *Toimintani*, II, 156; see also *ibid.*, pp. 161, 164, 202–203, 214, 220–221.

[35] Paasikivi, *Toimintani*, II, 202. The German Minister to Finland later asserted that Paasikivi was removed by the Finnish Government from his ministerial post. Wipert v. Blücher, *Suomen kohtalonaikoja—Muistelmia vuosilta 1935–44* (translated by Lauri Hirvensalo, Porvoo: Werner Söderström Osakeyhtiö, 1950), p. 224. It is quite possible that the Finnish Government told Blücher that Paasikivi had been dismissed, to gain favor in German eyes.

[36] Paasikivi, *Toimintani*, I, 97; Paasikivi, *Toimintani*, II, 219–221.

[37] Svento, *Ystäväni*, p. 17. The rarity of this understanding among educated Finns is a major theme of my article, "An Image of European Politics: The People's Patriotic Movement," *Journal of Central European Affairs*, XXII (October, 1962), 308–316.

[38] Svento, *Ystäväni*, p. 11.

have been reached at least several months earlier, before disastrous Finnish military reverses, on substantially better terms than were finally achieved.[39] The huge reparations schedule was but one price paid for a mistaken war.[40]

The lack of realism in Finnish foreign policy was particularly significant to Paasikivi because he shared Ranke's view of the primacy of foreign policy over domestic politics.[41] Paasikivi recognized the intimate interrelationship of domestic and international politics,[42] but nevertheless held that domestic political considerations should yield to the necessities of foreign policy.[43] The possibilities of domestic policy, especially for a small nation, were determined by international political developments. Indeed, the emergence of an independent Finnish political system had been possible only because of a favorable international constellation in 1917–1918.[44] The continued existence of that system depended upon international politics.[45] Even so powerful a nation as

[39] *Paasikiven muistelmia*, I, 78–79; *Paasikiven linja*, I, 57; Väinö Tanner, *Suomen tie rauhaan 1943–44* (Helsinki: Kustannusosakeyhtiö Tammi, 1952), p. 232.

[40] *Paasikiven linja*, I, 18.

[41] The classic formulation of this relationship was given by Ranke in his essay, "A Dialogue on Politics," translated by Theodore H. Von Laue, *Leopold Ranke: The Formative Years* (Princeton, 1950), pp. 172–173. Paasikivi's general evaluation of Ranke's significance was revealed when the former referred to "Ranke himself." Paasikivi, *Toimintani*, I, 96.

[42] *Paasikiven linja*, I, 89.

[43] *Ibid.*, pp. 13, 113, 187; *Paasikiven linja*, II, 124–125; Paasikivi, *Toimintani*, I, 59; Paasikivi, *Toimintani*, II, 185–186; Kekkonen and Tyyri, *Asiat*, p. 33; Kekkonen, "J. K. Paasikivi," p. 194; Pirkko Rommi, "Helmikuun manifestista Tarton rauhaan—J. K. Paasikiven Venäjän-politiikan perusteet," in Kare (editor), *J. K. Paasikivi*, pp. 39, 45. In spite of widespread acceptance in Finland since 1944 of Paasikivi's view in this matter, it is certainly exaggerated to argue that the primacy of foreign policy "has already become axiomatic" in Finnish politics, as does Jaakko Nousiainen, "The Parties and Foreign Policy," in *Finnish Foreign Policy: Studies in foreign politics* (Helsinki: Finnish Political Science Association, 1963), p. 180.

[44] *Paasikiven linja*, II, 22; *Paasikiven muistelmia*, I, 22; Paasikivi, *Toimintani*, II, 183, 185.

[45] Paasikivi, *Toimintani*, I, 36.

Weimar Germany saw the collapse of its political system because of its inability to solve its foreign policy problems.[46]

During his presidency Paasikivi placed overwhelming emphasis upon foreign policy. This emphasis flowed logically from his acceptance of the primacy of foreign policy. It would be only slight exaggeration to assert that as president he did not concern himself with domestic, particularly economic, policy.[47] His loyal follower, and successor in the presidency, Urho Kekkonen, went so far as to criticize Prime Minister Paasikivi for having virtually ignored the threat posed by inflation, which mounted to monumental proportions, during 1944-1946.[48] This failure to concern himself with economic policy was all the more notable in that Paasikivi was a former banker. The result of his concentration upon foreign policy was, however, that he exercised closer control over that policy than any other Finnish President.[49] The stress placed by Paasikivi upon foreign policy was similar to that placed by Konrad Adenauer as Chancellor of the German Federal Republic.[50]

In Paasikivi's view, foreign policy is much too difficult and complex to be decided by the man on the street. Leaders

[46] *Paasikiven linja*, II, 95; J. K. Paasikivi, *Kokoomuspuolueen valtiolliset periaatteet* (Helsinki: Suomalaisen Kirjallisuuden Seuran Kirjapainon Oy, 1936), p. 14.

[47] Mannerkorpi, "Tarton rauhasta," p. 78; Paavo Kastari, *Tasavallan presidentin asema* (Porvoo: Werner Söderström Osakeyhtiö, 1961), p. 73; Puntila, *Suomen poliittinen historia*, p. 214.

[48] Kekkonen, "J. K. Paasikivi," pp. 191-192; Urho Kekkonen, "J. K. Paasikivi," *Oma Maa* (1962), XI, p. 392.

[49] Jaakko Nousiainen, *Suomen poliittinen järestelmä* (Porvoo: Werner Söderström Osakeyhtiö, 1959), p. 267

[50] The political thought and action of these two men had several important similarities. Both achieved their greatest power in old age, after defeat of their nations in the Second World War, following long and distinguished careers at a less prominent level, and following a period of political retirement (1933-1945 for Adenauer and 1941-1944 for Paasikivi). Both concentrated upon foreign policy in the period of their greatest eminence—in particular, achieving reconciliation with the traditional enemy, now victorious (France for Adenauer and the Soviet Union for Paasikivi).

## J. K. PAASIKIVI 103

must boldly take responsibility upon themselves and guide public opinion in problems of foreign policy.[51] Paasikivi's boldness in this respect was unquestionable. He invariably called things by their appropriate names, repeatedly reminding the Finnish nation that it had lost two wars between 1939 and 1944.[52] He lost no opportunity to reiterate that these defeats necessitated adjustments in domestic politics as well as in foreign policy. Undoubtedly the most controversial of Paasikivi's public acts after 1944 were his attempts to influence domestic politics in directions he thought required by international politics.[53] In particular, Paasikivi's call in the 1945 parliamentary election campaign for "new faces" to replace outdated leaders in each party was later bitterly criticized.[54] The Prime Minister argued that policies are made by individual leaders, and new policies therefore demand new leaders.[55] This call was highly successful —the new Parliament of two hundred members contained ninety-two "new faces." [56]

One of the recurring questions in Finnish politics is whether Finland is Northern European or Eastern European. Paasikivi saw Finland as Northern European in culture, social structure, and national ideals.[57] Because he accepted the primacy of foreign policy, however, Paasikivi held that Finland was politically part of Eastern Europe.[58]

[51] Paasikivi, *Toimintani*, I, 118.
[52] Kurjensaari, "'Paasikiven aikakausi,'" p. 140.
[53] Yrjö Niiniluoto, *Suuri rooli—Suomen marsalkan, vapaaherra Carl Gustaf Emil Mannerheimin kirjallisen muotokuvan yritelmä* (Helsinki: Kustannusosakeyhtiö Otava, 1962), p. 51.
[54] Yrjö Soini, *Kuin Pietari hiilivalkealla—Sotasyyllisyysasian vaiheet 1944–1949* (Helsinki: Kustannusosakeyhtiö Otava, 1956), p. 55; Puntila, *Suomen poliittinen historia*, p. 210.
[55] *Paasikiven linja*, I, 15.
[56] Lauri Hyvämäki, *Vaaran vuodet 1944–48* (Helsinki: Kustannusosakeyhtiö Otava, 1957), p. 54.
[57] Paasikivi, *Toimintani*, II, 191–192.
[58] *Ibid.*, p. 7; Paasikivi, *Toimintani*, I, 5, 54; *Paasikiven muistelmia*, I, 124–125, 128, 136; *Paasikiven muistelmia*, II, 9, 160, 192, 199, 201; *Paasikiven linja*, I, 9, 13–14, 29, 125; Rommi, "Helmikuun manifestista," p. 52.

The fundamental fact of Finnish politics was the geographical proximity of one of the great powers. In this perception Paasikivi was undoubtedly correct. As a political (rather than a religious, cultural, or economic) area, Eastern Europe consists of those nations for whom the relationship with Russia has been the most important single fact. There is no doubt that the union of Sweden and Finland before 1809 remains of considerable political importance for the latter. So long as Russian expansionism in Northern Europe was a vital force, however, Finland's status as the last province of the Swedish Kingdom was insecure. After becoming a Grand Duchy of the Russian Emperor, Finland was able to maintain its remarkable autonomy only at the will of its Grand Duke. The Russian Revolution led to Finnish independence. Even independence did not reduce the significance of Russian attitudes toward the Finns, as the wars of 1939–1944 demonstrated. Paasikivi was therefore on firm ground when he insisted on the priority of the need for good relations with the Soviet Union.

Less certain, however, is the justification for Paasikivi's optimism concerning the possibility of good Russo-Finnish relations It is remarkable that a man whose personal *Weltanschauung* was based upon a sense of tragic pessimism [59] was an optimist concerning this possibility.[60] Because he

[59] *Paasikiven linja*, I, 59–60, 94, 115, 169, 185, 202; *Paasikiven linja*, II, 35, 66, 187, 193, 200, 252–253; *Paasikiven muistelmia*, I, 35, 37, 39, 81, 84; *Paasikiven muistelmia*, II, 160, 191, 193–194, 197, 199–200, 202; Paasikivi, *Toimintani*, I, 7, 9, 13, 15, 29, 71, 128, 131, 148, 165, 199, 207–208; Paasikivi, *Toimintani*, II, 82, 177–178, 193, 202; Arvi Korhonen, "Paasikivi Moskovassa," *Suomalainen Suomi*, December, 1958, p. 557; Kekkonen, "J. K. Paasikivi—rauhantekijä-presidentti," p. 189; Puntila, *J. K. Paasikiven linja*, p. 8; Kekkonen and Tyyri, *Asiat*, pp. 93–94; Kauko Kare, "Snellmanin perintö, in Kare (editor), *J. K. Paasikivi*, p. 35; Rommi, "Helmikuun manifestista," p. 46; Mannerkorpi, "Tarton rauhasta," p. 65; Pentti Poukka, "Talouspoliitikko Paasikivi," in Kare (editor), *J. K. Paasikivi*, p. 122; G. A. Gripenberg, *Lontoo-Vatikaani-Tukholma—Suomalaisen diplomaatin muistelmia* (translated by Lauri Karén, Porvoo: Werner Söderström Osakeyhtiö, 1960), pp. 308, 310.

[60] *Paasikiven linja*, I, 27; *Paasikiven muistelmia*, I, 61, 117; *Paasikiven muistelmia*, II, 198–199.

was an optimist about Russo-Finnish relations, Paasikivi was also an optimist about the future of Finnish independence.[61] This optimism was based upon the explicit assumption of the compatibility of Russian and Finnish national interest.[62] The essential justification, in Paasikivi's view, for this assumption was the existence of good relations between Russia and Finland between 1809 and 1899, before Russification attempts began.[63] Paasikivi, like other members of the generation of older conservatives, was far from antagonistic toward the Imperial Russia of his political youth. After 1917, it was by no means certain that the foreign policy goals of the Soviet Government were the same as those of the Imperial Government. Paasikivi's assumption of the identity of Russian and Finnish national interest was irrelevant if Soviet motivation was not based on national interest. In this respect, Paasikivi firmly believed that the Soviet Union "despite its internal changes was in reality the same old Russia," [64] and that it was national interest, not permanent revolution, which motivated Soviet foreign policy, including that toward Finland.[65] The "Paasikivi line" can be defined as a way of communicating with the Russians.[66] Unlike most other Finnish political leaders, Paasikivi's command of the Russian language was complete.[67] His favorite literary works were the writings of Gogol.[68] It is less certain, however, whether Paasikivi ever spoke, or

[61] Svento, *Ystäväni*, p. 55.

[62] *Paasikiven linja*, I, 30–31, 205, 213–214; *Paasikiven muistelmia*, I, 126; *Paasikiven muistelmia*, II, 175–176, 178, 180–181, 197–199; Paasikivi, *Toimintani*, I, 53, 93, 214; Paasikivi, *Toimintani*, II, 3, 53, 57, 128, 175, 191, 201.

[63] *Paasikiven linja*, I, 73–74, 91; *Paasikiven linja*, II, 20; *Paasikiven muistelmia*, I, 28, 100, 127; Sukselainen, "A Statesman's Life," p. 35.

[64] Paasikivi, *Toimintani*, I, 16; see also *ibid.*, p. 33; Paasikivi, *Toimintani*, II, 136.

[65] Paasikivi, *Toimintani*, I, 34, 92–93, 213; Paasikivi, *Toimintani*, II, 52, 136–137.

[66] Kekkonen and Tyyri, *Asiat*, pp. 78–79.

[67] Laati, "Rauhanneuvottelija Paasikivi," p. 85; Svento, *Ystäväni*, p. 58.

[68] *Paasikiven linja*, I, 185; *Paasikiven muistelmia*, I, 30; Tanner, "J. K. Paasikivi," p. 480.

even understood, the language of the new Soviet politics. Although Soviet leaders correctly regarded him as "a capitalist" and "bourgeois," Paasikivi recognized the importance of achieving and maintaining good personal relations with these leaders. He never forgot that the personal attitude of the Grand Duke had been a major factor in preserving Finnish autonomy throughout the nineteenth century.[69] Paasikivi succeeded remarkably well in his attempt to keep channels of communication open with Soviet leaders. During the Winter War Väinö Tanner told the German Minister to Finland—not without a touch of sarcasm—that Paasikivi was *persona grata* in Moscow, while Tanner was not.[70] This was correct. During his ministry in Moscow 1940–1941 Paasikivi was one of the few foreign representatives on good terms with Soviet leaders, including even Molotov.[71] Partly because they shared an earthy sense of humor, Paasikivi and Stalin were on especially friendly terms.[72] When Paasikivi left Moscow in the spring of 1941 Stalin presented him with a personal gift: a large shipment of wheat for the hard-pressed Finns.[73] During the presidential election campaign of 1940 Molotov told Paasikivi that the Soviet Government would gladly see him elected.[74] These harmonious contacts continued after Stalin's death.[75] In 1954 Paasikivi was

[69] *Paasikiven muistelmia*, I, 27–28.

[70] Blücher, *Suomen kohtalonaikoja*, p. 181.

[71] Paasikivi, *Toimintani*, I, 39; Paasikivi, *Toimintani*, II, 2–3, 16, 18, 40, 66–67, 78–79, 147, 163, 178, 216; Grigore Gafencu, *Prelude to the Russian Campaign: From the Moscow Pact (August 21st 1939) to the opening of hostilities in Russia (June 22nd 1941)* (translated by E. Fletcher-Allen, London, 1945), pp. 111–112, 207.

[72] Blücher, *Suomen kohtalonaikoja*, p. 363; Gripenberg, *Lontoo*, p. 304; Laati, "Rauhanneuvottelija Paasikivi," p. 99.

[73] Paasikivi, *Toimintani*, II, 216–218. Paasikivi, in turn, regarded Stalin as "a comfortable man to get on with, a man with a sense of humor." *Life*, March 4, 1940, p. 10; see also *Paasikiven linja*, I, 27, 74, 187; Paasikivi, *Toimintani*, I, 31, 38, 49, 69, 94–95, 211–212; Paasikivi, *Toimintani*, II, 5–6, 74–75, 183; Svento, *Ystäväni*, pp. 30–31.

[74] Paasikivi, *Toimintani*, II, 129–130; see also Hirvikallio, *Tasavallan presidentin vaalit*, p. 90. Paasikivi had already withdrawn his name from consideration.

[75] Svento, *Ystäväni*, p. 58.

awarded the highest Soviet decoration, the Order of Lenin.[76] A high-ranking delegation of Soviet officials attended his funeral in December, 1956.[77]

Even if Soviet foreign policy was in fact motivated by national interest, and the latter was compatible with Finnish national interest, there was always the possibility that Soviet policy makers, however amiable personally, might mistakenly perceive their national interest in a particular situation, with fatal consequences for Finnish independence. As Paasikivi conceded, the definition of national interest in a particular situation is inevitably subjective.[78] The future of Finnish independence thus rested upon the rationality of Soviet policy toward Finland. Paasikivi's assumption of such rationality conflicted with important elements of his political thought. He argued, for instance, not only that the foreign policy of all great powers is selfish, but that this selfishness is narrow and short-sighted in practice.[79] An example of this lack of vision was the attempt to Russify Finland after 1899; this attempt was an expression of irrational forces which incorrectly interpreted Russian national interest in Finland.[80] Irrationality is not confined to the leaders of one or all great powers, however. All men gladly confuse hope and truth.[81] Irrationality is a universal type of inadequacy of political judgment.[82] In an irrational world, the preconditions for thought and discussion are absent.[83] Like other conservatives, Paasikivi was a misanthrope.[84] His pessimism was

[76] E. Ambartsumov, "Soviet-Finnish Relations—Relations of Peace and Friendship," *International Affairs* (Moscow), October, 1955, p. 51.

[77] Kurjensaari, "'Paasikiven aikakausi,'" p. 145.

[78] Paasikivi, *Toimintani*, I, 35, 53; Paasikivi, *Toimintani*, II, 182.

[79] *Paasikiven muistelmia*, I, 81; *Paasikiven muistelmia*, II, 189; Paasikivi, *Toimintani*, I, 54, 173.

[80] *Paasikiven muistelmia*, I, 83–84, 100; *Paasikiven muistelmia*, II, 197–198.

[81] Paasikivi, *Toimintani*, I, 101.

[82] *Ibid.*, pp. 12, 35–36; *Paasikiven linja*, I, 169; *Paasikiven linja*, II, 73–74, 216–217; Paasikivi, *Valtio*, pp. 40–42; Paasikivi, *Toimintani*, II, 118.

[83] Paasikivi, *Toimintani*, I, 54.

[84] *Paasikiven muistelmia*, I, 61, 148, 150–151, 182; Paasikivi, *Toimintani*, I, 116; Paasikivi, *Toimintani*, II, 14, 118; Heikkilä, *Paasikivi*, p. 105.

thus pessimism about human nature. Today men cry "Hosanna!" and tomorrow they cry "Crucify Him!" [85] Because of the inconstancy of human nature history is neither logical nor consistent.[86]

Nowhere was the inconstancy of human nature more clearly evident in Finnish politics than in the political isolation in which Paasikivi lived before 1944, contrasted with the almost universal praise in which he basked after that year. Paasikivi never changed his attitude toward Russia once it was formed during his student years, but the Finnish nation did. Before 1944, it was widely assumed that Paasikivi was dangerously "soft" on Russia, and he was therefore not popular among Finns in general, and even among his fellow members of the (Conservative) National Coalition Party.[87] Paasikivi recognized that his firmness toward Soviet demands was suspect among other Finnish leaders at the times when they depended upon him to extricate Finland from an impossible situation in diplomatic negotiations with the Soviet Union.[88] This recognition led him to request that Väinö Tanner—of whose firmness toward the Soviet Union there was no doubt—accompany him on his missions to Moscow in the autumn of 1939.[89] Foreign Minister Erkko[90] wrote privately to Tanner: "If only P. won't fall on his knees." [91] Paasikivi's own party declined to support him in the 1940 presidential election because of his attitude toward

[85] *Paasikiven muistelmia*, I, 150.
[86] *Ibid.*, p. 21.
[87] *Paasikiven linja*, I, 196; *Paasikiven muistelmia*, I, 9; Kekkonen and Tyyri, *Asiat*, pp. 117–118, 124.
[88] Paasikivi, *Toimintani*, II, 156, 160.
[89] Paasikivi, *Toimintani*, I, 56; Mannerkorpi, "Tarton rauhasta," p. 66. The circumstances, if not the political significance, of Tanner's membership in the Finnish delegation were misunderstood by the German Minister to Finland. Blücher, *Suomen kohtalonaikoja*, pp. 157–158.
[90] As publisher of Finland's largest newspaper, Erkko in this case not only reflected, but also had helped to create, public opinion.
[91] Väinö Tanner, *Olin ulkoministerinä talvisodan aikana* (Helsinki: Kustannusosakeyhtiö Tammi, 1950), p. 95.

J. K. PAASIKIVI 109

the Soviet Union.⁹² Before that election, T. M. Kivimäki, a leader of the (liberal) National Progressive Party, privately assured the German Government that Paasikivi would not be elected.⁹³ The German Minister to Finland was informed by the Finnish Foreign Minister during the spring of 1941 that Paasikivi, as Finnish Minister to the Soviet Union, lacked his superior's confidence.⁹⁴ After 1944, denunciations of Paasikivi's alleged servility toward Russia were made by both Finns ⁹⁵ and foreigners.⁹⁶

The assertion that Paasikivi was "soft" on Russia was manifestly unfair to him. Servility was no more characteristic of him than of Mannerheim, Tanner, or Ståhlberg. Paasikivi drew a clear line between peripheral matters, in which a small power wisely conceded whatever was legitimately demanded by a great power, and questions of principle, in which even a small power was obligated to stand firm. Finland should respond to all Russian demands with a willingness to discuss differences in the hope of reaching a negotiated, mutually acceptable settlement. If such a settlement could not be reached—but only then—Finns would have to say, with Luther: "Here I stand; I can do no other. God help me." ⁹⁷ Along with his fellow Old Finns, Paasikivi felt that the line had been passed by the Russification demands of 1909, and therefore resigned from the Finnish

⁹² Paavo Hirvikallio, *Tasavallan presidentin vaalit Suomessa 1919–1950* (Helsinki: Werner Söderström Osakeyhtiö, 1958), pp. 88–89.

⁹³ *Ibid.*, p. 93.

⁹⁴ Blücher, *Suomen kohtalonaikoja*, p. 224.

⁹⁵ Jussi Talvi, *Hyvä on elämä—Romaani* (Helsinki: Kustannusosakeyhtiö Otava, 1956), p. 303; Jussi Talvi, *Yksi miljoonista—Romaani* (Helsinki: Kustannusosakeyhtiö Otava, 1959), pp. 351, 363.

⁹⁶ The most vigorous blast of all against Gustaf Mannerheim and J. K. Paasikivi came from an American observer, who said of "the regime which has been emerging since the fall of 1944": "liberty and justice within the law have been largely replaced by the arbitrary compulsions exerted by Russia and applied by Finnish communists who bask in the Eastern sun and do the work of the Kremlin." John H. Wuorinen (editor), *Finland and World War II: 1939–1944* (New York, 1948), p. 20.

⁹⁷ *Paasikiven muistelmia*, I, 2; see also *ibid.*, p. 77.

Cabinet.⁹⁸ In his Independence Day speech of December, 1944, Prime Minister Paasikivi eloquently stated the support of all Finns, regardless of party, for continued national independence as the minimum Finns would expect of the Soviet Union.⁹⁹ Below this minimum Paasikivi was not willing to go.¹⁰⁰

Because he refused to sacrifice Finnish independence, but also because he was willing to yield on secondary matters, by the end of his political career it was evident that Paasikivi was the greatest statesman that independent Finland had produced.¹⁰¹ The Mannerheim Line, which consisted only of a few scattered pillboxes, proved remarkably effective during the Winter War; the "Paasikivi line," which consisted only of political realism, proved equally effective after 1944. Without the former, the latter would have been impossible. Without the latter, the former would have been meaningless. It may be true that the Mannerheim Line was the one thin line that separated civilization from savagery,¹⁰² but it was the "Paasikivi line" which saved Finland from self-destruction.

As a playgoer, Paasikivi realized that *sorti* is just as important as *entre*.¹⁰³ The Paasikivi era in Finnish politics had begun unpromisingly enough, but it ended with substantial promise for the future. The final months of Paasikivi's presidency saw Finland finally able to join the United Nations

---

⁹⁸ *Paasikiven muistelmia*, II, 74–93; see also *ibid.*, p. 11; John H. Hodgson, "Finland's Position in the Russian Empire, 1905–1910," *Journal of Central European Affairs*, XX (July, 1960), 158–173; John H. Hodgson, "The Paasikivi Line," *The American Slavic and East European Review*, XVIII (April, 1959), 145–173.
⁹⁹ *Paasikiven linja*, I, 10.
¹⁰⁰ Svento, *Ystäväni*, pp. 65–66; Tauno Suontausta, "'Paasikiven sopimus' —eduskunnan sopimus. Vuoden 1948 ystävyyssopimuksen taustaa ja sovellusta," in Kare (editor), *J. K. Paasikivi*, p. 103.
¹⁰¹ C. Leonard Lundin, *Finland in the Second World War* (Bloomington, 1957), p. 25; Kurjensaari, *Jäähyväiset*, p. 315.
¹⁰² Rosita Forbes, *These Men I Knew* (New York, 1940), p. 276.
¹⁰³ *Paasikiven linja*, I, 198.

J. K. PAASIKIVI 111

Organization and the Nordic Council. Porkkala, leased to the Soviet Union in 1944 for use as a naval base, was returned prematurely to Finland. The last of these accomplishments was announced while Paasikivi was on a trip to Moscow in September, 1955. With the return of Porkkala, the pen repaired what the sword had broken.[104] The contrast between Paasikivi's trips to Moscow in 1939 and 1955 was vividly apparent to all.[105] The return of Porkkala was undoubtedly the peak of Paasikivi's political career; because he was a politician in politics, it was also the greatest moment of his long life. As he prepared to retire, Paasikivi expressed deep satisfaction with the world about him.[106] A few months after this retirement, Finns busy with Christmas preparations took time off to bury him, and to express their satisfaction with him. Some Finns perhaps even remembered another kind of Christmas, in 1939.

The relatively long age of parties of individual notables [107] was finally ended in Finnish politics, and the age of bureaucratic mass parties, of which Väinö Tanner was the precursor, had finally triumphed. Political leadership in Finland would never be the same. Whether it would ever again be a stage for heroes was doubtful. This fact undoubtedly had its advantages—especially for those who were not heroes. Personal responsibility, as Mannerheim had sadly noted, no longer mattered as much as before. Whether col-

[104] Ibid., p. 193; see also ibid., p. 186.
[105] Kai Brunila, Porkkala on meidän—Jälkikatsaus sanoin ja kuvin (translated by Lauri Hirvensalo, Porvoo: Werner Söderström Osakeyhtiö, 1956), pp. 64, 66.
[106] Paasikiven linja, I, 176–177, 192, 195, 205–206, 208–209, 213–214; Paasikiven muistelmia, I, 32, 77. It is inconceivable that Paasikivi would have agreed with, or even understood, the following statement: "Political leadership is a full-time career with little opportunity for relaxation or cultivation of other interests. In retrospect few intelligent men who have enjoyed power have felt that its rewards were commensurate with the personal sacrifices it entailed." Sidney Hook, The Hero in History: A Study in Limitation and Possibility (Boston, 1957), p. 24.
[107] Paasikiven muistelmia, I, 185; K. J. Ståhlberg, Parlamentarismi Suomen valtiosäännössä (Helsinki: Kustannusosakeyhtiö Otava, 1927), p. 69.

lective responsibility can be meaningful or feasible in politics has not yet been established. It is perhaps worth noting that the greatest of all students of bureaucracy concluded:

> The honor of the political leader, of the leading statesman . . . lies precisely in an exclusive *personal* responsibility for what he does, a responsibility he cannot and must not reject or transfer.[108]

[108] H. H. Gerth and C. Wright Mills (editors), *From Max Weber: Essays in Sociology* (New York, 1958), p. 95.

## VI
✪✪✪✪
## Finnish Politics as a Vocation

The greatest of all political leaders once observed: "If you would be a leader of men, you must lead your own generation, not the next."[1] Like most aphorisms, Wilson's glittering generalization is initially impressive, and Wilson's own experience in 1919 provides strong evidence for its accuracy. Certainly politics is always concerned with action in the present, but it is also concerned with action in the past and action in the future. As Wilson himself discovered, the burden of the past—not only conscious policy decisions— limits what can be done today. What is done today, in turn, limits what can be done tomorrow. What is left undone today is often the task of politics tomorrow. Unfinished agendas are not uncommon in politics, and yesterday's leaders are today's heroes or villains. This was the ultimate meaning of Wilson's own political career, as a skeptical biographer realized: "Wilson's triumph was as a teacher, his lesson written in the copybooks of generations unborn when he taught."[2]

The four Finns studied in this book are all dead now. To many persons, including perhaps most political scientists, this makes them part of history, not politics. The preceding pages should have demonstrated, however, that the successes and failures of these four men are intimately involved

[1] Woodrow Wilson, *Leaders of Men* (edited by T. H. Vail Motter, Princeton, 1952), p. 29.
[2] John Morton Blum, *Woodrow Wilson and the Politics of Morality* (Boston, 1956), p. 199.

with the present reality of Finnish politics. One can never wipe the slate completely clean in politics, and this is especially true of a nation so tradition-oriented as the Finnish. The fundamental facts of present-day Finnish politics—national independence and parliamentary government—would be inconceivable without the personal contributions—sometimes unwilling—of these four men. In this sense they were all, to use Sidney Hook's useful distinction,[3] event-making, rather than merely eventful, men. The events they made will influence tomorrow as well as today. It may well be that they have helped in large measure to chart the course of future Finnish politics. That yesterday's political leaders have a message for tomorrow as well as for yesterday and today is, indeed, what ordinary people mean to convey when they award the title statesman.

Each of these four Finns was deeply concerned with the way future generations of Finns would view him. Since they all lived to be octagenarians, they all had ample opportunity to play the role of elder statesmen. All except Ståhlberg published extensive memoirs, which were essentially self-justifications, and even Ståhlberg assiduously saw to it that his voluminous speeches were published and kept in print. Tanner's memoirs were the most defensive—one volume, dealing with 1918, was entitled "How It Really Happened" —perhaps because he was in prison as a "war-responsible" when he started on his enormous publication project. Paasikivi's memoirs, incomparable sources for the history of Finnish politics, are stylistically elegant appeals for permanent Finnish adherence to the Paasikivi line. All four Finns practiced what Mannerheim explicitly preached when he asked: ". . . had not my countrymen a right to hear my interpretation of the causes that had led to the position where Finland now stood? . . . it is my hope that the essence of the experiences and lessons life has given me will

[3] Sidney Hook, *The Hero in History: A Study in Limitation and Possibility* (Boston, 1957), pp. 151–183.

enlighten and guide those generations upon whose shoulders Finland's welfare in the future will rest."[4]

All four men were clearly appealing for supporters in the future. It is therefore fair as well as necessary to assess their probable relative appeal to future generations of Finns. Inevitably this involves judgments that cannot be documented, but perhaps the most important questions are always those which cannot be answered definitively. Finns in the future will see the past of Finnish politics in terms of their own needs and desires, their own hopes and fears. If every generation of Europeans will have its own Lenin, its own Hitler, and its own Churchill, every generation of Finns will have its own Mannerheim, its own Tanner, its own Ståhlberg, and its own Paasikivi. This fact is a demonstration of the stature of these men. Some Finns will act to preserve what they perceive to be the strengths of the past, and some—not necessarily other—Finns will act to destroy what they perceive to be the weaknesses of the past. If the argument of this book is correct, the strengths and weaknesses of Mannerheim, Tanner, Ståhlberg, and Paasikivi will be a large part of the strengths and weaknesses of the Finnish political past.

Future generations of Finns are quite likely, it seems to the present author, to view Finnish politics in the first half of the twentieth century as characterized by too much conflict and too little cooperation. Linguistic and class conflict within Finland and international conflict with the Soviet Union will probably be regarded as unfortunate and perhaps as unnecessary. These three areas of conflict are likely to provide the essential bases for evaluation of the political leaders studied in this book.

Of these three areas of conflict the linguistic will undoubtedly be viewed as the least important. The rights of the Finnish-language majority and the rights of the Swedish-

[4] *The Memoirs of Marshal Mannerheim* (translated by Count Eric Lewenhaupt, New York, 1954), p. xi.

language minority are at the present time clearly established realities in Finnish politics, and there is no reason to assume there will be any important change in this situation. On the whole, Finns of both languages have slowly and painfully learned since 1899 that what unites them is more significant than what divides them. Bilingual Finland is in fact one nation, with a common past and a common destiny. This fact was realized earlier by Mannerheim, Tanner, Ståhlberg, and Paasikivi than by the majority of Finns. In this respect they all served to advance the cause of linguistic reconciliation. None was identified with either Swedish-language or Finnish-language extremism. As a young man Ståhlberg vigorously supported the cause of the then-disadvantaged Finnish-language majority, but when that struggle had been won, he wrote effective guarantees for the Swedish-language minority into the Constitution of 1919. Tanner never really cared about the language question, and as a result helped to make the Finnish Social Democratic Party bilingual. For all practical purposes Paasikivi ignored the language question, as he ignored most problems of domestic politics. Even Mannerheim's pathetic attempt to learn Finnish late in life is likely to be viewed indulgently by Finnish-speaking Finns as a sign of honorable intentions.

More important to future generations of Finns will be the responsibility of these four men for the bitterness of the class struggle in Finnish politics during the first half of the twentieth century. The Civil War of 1918 is the great tragic event in modern Finnish politics, and to a considerable degree the future evaluation of these four men will rest upon their participation in, and their reaction to, that event. Ståhlberg will undoubtedly come out best in this respect. His hands were clean in 1918, and he spent much of the rest of his life trying to reconcile the vanquished and the victors of 1918. To a considerable degree his attempt was successful, and what political stability has characterized Finland since 1918 is his monument. He taught the working class that a middle-class politician could work for, and achieve, social justice, and he taught the middle class the more difficult lesson that a middle-class politician should work for, and achieve, social justice. Tanner taught the working class after 1918 that social justice could be achieved without violence. In late 1917 and early 1918, however, Tanner had sat on the sidelines, waiting to pick up the pieces of the Social Democratic Party after the workers' revolt inevitably failed, without trying to teach the working class anything. Paasikivi's attitude toward the Civil War was essentially similar in its passivity to Tanner's. Paasikivi did nothing to fan the flames of middle-class violence, but when the Civil Guards had triumphed, he willingly accepted the prime ministership in May, 1918. Before and after 1918, however, Paasikivi proved surprisingly receptive to social justice—provided it was necessary to gain support for his foreign-policy goals—for a wealthy banker. The biggest loser in terms of 1918 will continue to be Mannerheim. The triumph of his Civil Guards was a hollow victory, and the strength of the Finnish Communist Party today and in the foreseeable future is a lasting testimonial to his errors in 1918. Mannerheim never believed in the desirability of social justice, but as an aristocrat his contempt for the middle class matched his contempt for the working class. Both classes were, however, good cannon fodder for the greater glory of Gustaf Mannerheim. Finnish nationalists—for all practical purposes, all Finns—will in the future increasingly understand that for Mannerheim the Finnish nation was a means rather than an end, possessing at most instrumental value, not inherent value. He yearned passionately for yesterday, and there can be little doubt that he did all he could to restore the old regime in Finland as elsewhere in Europe, but in his crusade against Bolshevism he unintentionally helped to preserve Finnish independence.

Because he never intentionally did anything which harmed his conception of the legitimate national interest of Russia, Mannerheim may not appeal to the nationalist in every Finn. Mannerheim's lack of nationalism, however, made him able in 1944 to lead Finns toward a reconciliation with the Soviet Union. This was his greatest achievement in Finnish politics, and this will be the greatest single element in his appeal to future generations of Finns. Finns today are justifiably tired of war with the Soviet Union, and there is little reason to assume that the foreseeable future will see any change in this sentiment. Indeed, the most important single Finnish policy goal for many decades is likely to be the continuation of good Finnish-Soviet relations. For his part in the new policy of 1944–1946, Mannerheim will probably gain in stature in the eyes of Finns, especially as 1918 recedes in distance. The greatest beneficiary in this respect will continue to be Paasikivi, however. The "Paasikivi era" will be seen, perhaps for some decades, as the golden era of Finnish politics, and he will be *the* hero for most Finns. Throughout his lifetime he believed in the possibility of a peaceful Finnish foreign policy, and in 1944 his time came. The Paasikivi line has been an enormous success, and therefore its chief opponent, Tanner, has been discredited; as long as it remains a success, Tanner's stock will continue to go down. The dichotomy between Tanner's contributions in domestic politics and his failures in foreign policy will continue to grow in the eyes of most Finns. If he had died in 1939, Tanner would have been a hero; after 1939 his growing obsession with demonstrating his opposition to the Soviet Union increasingly made him a villain. Since his personal responsibility for leading Finland into the wars of 1939–1940 and 1941–1944 is greater than that of any other Finn, this decline in his reputation is perhaps justifiable. Ståhlberg, who was just as strongly anti-Russian as Tanner, had the good fortune not to hold public office during or after the Second World War, and *his* reputation was therefore not tarnished. For Ståhlberg, at least some of the concessions Finland had to make to the Soviet Union after 1944 were unconstitutional. Given his overwhelming devotion to constitutionalism, and the fact that the Finnish Constitution was—and is—his personal creation, it is highly unlikely that Ståhlberg, if he had been in office after 1944, would have been as flexible as Mannerheim and Paasikivi, neither of them legalists, proved to be. That Tanner's reputation declined, and Ståhlberg's did not, suggests that even event-making men are also made by events.

Because Finns are increasingly recognizing the primacy of foreign policy over domestic politics, Mannerheim and Paasikivi will grow in importance as guides for the future, and Tanner and Ståhlberg will fall by the wayside. Tanner's fall from grace will not cause many tears, especially since it is his type of bureaucratic party leader to whom the future of Finnish domestic politics belongs, and it is exceedingly difficult to feel compassion for bureaucrats. Furthermore, Tanner's next-of-kin, the Finnish Social Democratic Party, survives. Ståhlberg's party, the National Progressive Party, perhaps unfortunately for Finnish politics, did not even survive its creator, dying one year before Ståhlberg. The institutional framework of parliamentary government, on whose creation Ståhlberg lavished such loving attention in 1919, still lives, nevertheless, and is likely to be present as long as there is an independent Finnish political system. In this sense, Ståhlberg's lessons will still be taught, even though not every Finnish politician will remember who wrote the textbook.

If the future belongs to Mannerheim and Paasikivi, it does not belong to them equally. Both of them taught the necessity of good relations with the Soviet Union, but there was an important difference. For Mannerheim Finnish independence was not the highest of all political values, but for Paasikivi it was. Concessions to the Soviet Union were justified for Paasikivi only if they helped assure future Finnish independence. Finland's territory might be smaller, and its aspirations more limited after 1944 than in interwar years, but Paasikivi felt, probably correctly, that its independence rested on a more secure foundation. In quoting Luther's famous declaration of intransigence, Paasikivi revealed the religious fervor with which he held to Finnish independence. Such a fervor would have been inconceivable in Mannerheim, for whom nationalism was one of the many sins of modernity. Since nationalism is and will remain the organizing principle of Finnish politics, it was Paasikivi, not Mannerheim, who expressed the highest aspirations of the Finnish people. He achieved greatness not only by his uniqueness as a human being—no one who ever saw or heard J. K. Paasikivi would ever mistake him for anyone else—but by being, in spite of his philosophical disdain for the masses, genuinely representative of the deeper needs and tendencies of his fellow Finns, so that in following him they did, they do, and they will truly express themselves. Paasikivi would doubtless have recognized himself in a portrait of the politician in politics:

> It is immensely moving when a *mature man*—no matter whether young or old in years—is aware of a responsibility for the consequences of his conduct and really feels such responsibility with heart and soul. He then acts by following an ethic of responsibility and somewhere he reaches the point where he says: 'Here I stand; I can do no other.' That is something genuinely human and moving. And every one of us who is not spiritually dead must realize the possibility of finding himself at some time in that position. In so far as this is true, an ethic of ultimate ends and an ethic of responsibility are not absolute contrasts but rather supplements, which only in unison constitute a genuine man—a man who *can* have the 'calling for politics.' [5]

It was, in the end, neither a cosmopolite general, nor an efficient organization man, nor a genteel scholar, but a hot-tempered, foul-mouthed old banker who taught Finns—and others—what it means to have Finnish politics as a vocation.

---

[5] H. H. Gerth and C. Wright Mills (editors), *From Max Weber: Essays in Sociology* (New York, 1958), p. 127.